No. 12 of The Pegasus Books edited by
PATRICK PRINGLE

THE PEGASUS BOOK OF ARCHAEOLOGY

THE PEGASUS BOOK OF
ARCHAEOLOGY

by

GEOFFREY PALMER
and
NOEL LLOYD

Illustrated by
David Killick

LONDON
DENNIS DOBSON

First published in Great Britain 1968
by Dobson Books Ltd, 80 Kensington Church Street,
London, W.8
Printed in Great Britain by
Bristol Typesetting Co, Ltd,
Barton Manor, St Philips, Bristol 2
SBN 234 77996 9

CONTENTS

CHAPTER ONE

FLINT TOOLS OR FAKES?

'THE WORLD', declared James Ussher, Archbishop of Armagh in the early seventeenth century, 'was created in the year 4004 B.C. This I have calculated from evidence I found in the Old Testament.'

That statement appeared in his book *Annals of the Ancient and New Testaments* in 1650. It was so widely believed that the date appeared in the margin of the Authorized Version of the Bible. It still appears in some editions!

Dr John Lightfoot, Vice-Chancellor of the University of Cambridge, was bold enough to go even further than the Archbishop.

'Heaven and earth . . . were created all together . . . and man was created by the Trinity on October 23, 4004 B.C.,' he wrote; adding the impressive detail, 'at nine o'clock in the morning.'

Such extraordinary assertions would take our breath away if they were made today by a responsible scholar or scientist, though there are people who still believe the earth is flat. In the late seventeenth and eighteenth centuries the idea that man had a long history before written records began was held only by a few cranks or outsiders.

In those days prehistoric stone tools were often called

9

'thunder-stones', 'elf-darts' or 'fairy arrows'. That they could have been made by human beings was unthinkable. When they were found in association with the remains of extinct animals—well, it was either accident or plain fraud.

When cranks such as Mercati at the end of the sixteenth century, de la Payrere in the middle of the seventeenth, John Frere at the end of the eighteenth, and in the early nineteenth a number of scientists from England, France and Belgium, put forward the idea that early man had lived at the same time as the mammoth, cave-bear and woolly rhinoceros, in a remote period 'beyond that of the present world' as John Frere said, they were met by polite disbelief, laughter or scorn.

This is the story of the man who broke the chilling circle of indifference and smashed the complacency of the experts . . .

Jacques Boucher de Crêvecoeur de Perthes was a Frenchman of no great learning or scientific training who was the head of the Customs House at Abbeville, near the mouth of the River Somme. There was nothing in his background to suggest that he would become one of the great researchers of his time, though his father was a botanist and fostered his son's interest in natural history.

De Perthes had a keen, observing eye and a logical, independent mind. He did not believe the Genesis story of Adam and Eve, but thought that mankind had started in a crude and primitive way, a long time before the Flood, and that history was a slow evolutionary process.

Cuvier, the great French naturalist, had said, with such authority that few dared contradict him, that fossil man did not exist. The truth was that fossil man had not been found. With that thought uppermost in his mind Boucher de Perthes went to work.

From an archaeological point of view his story begins in 1837, when he was forty-nine years old. After nine years, during which he had searched in vain for evidence of fossil man in gravel-pits and the deposits laid down by rivers, he found, in a gravel-bed near his own house at Abbeville, a piece of chipped flint about six inches long. Soon afterwards he found another, then a third—all roughly the same size and shape. This was more than coincidence, surely? These were prehistoric knives . . .

Archaeologists to whom he showed his finds were sceptical. Accidents of nature, they called them, and handed them back with indulgent smiles.

De Perthes was not put off by their dismissal. He hired workmen to help him, offering two francs for each article they found, and the search continued.

It took a long time for his enthusiasm and determination to get across to the men working for him, but eventually they became as keen as he was. Gradually there grew an enormous collection of what de Perthes called 'antediluvian [before the Flood] objects', which we now know belonged to the Stone Age. It was so great that he had to build a museum on to the side of his house to store them all.

The museum contained more than a thousand hand-axes, a large number of arrow-heads, knives and worked bones, many of them from the river-laid gravels of the Somme valley. They had been found deep down in the same layers as the bones of prehistoric elephants and rhinoceroses. Some of the artifacts were roughly made, some were smooth and polished, and they were all of stone or bone, fashioned before the use of metals had been known.

He offered his vast collection to a Paris museum, but to his intense disappointment the authorities were not interested and his offer was refused. Had not Cuvier said there was no such thing as fossil man? Therefore there could be no tools made by such people. De Perthes had collected nothing but a lot of rubbish. So said the men from the museum.

The year was now 1847, and de Perthes published the first volume of a three-volume work called *Celtic and Antediluvian Antiquities,* which described his ten years' work.

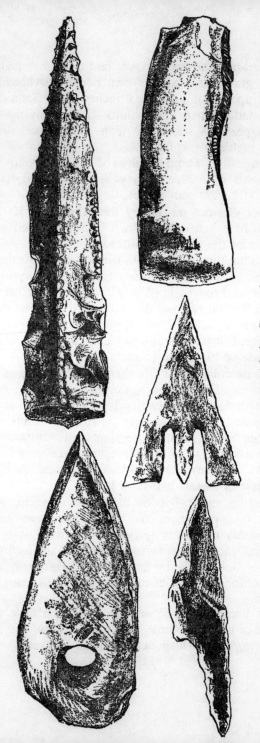

Tools and weapons of the Stone Age

The book did not please the critics. The general opinion was that de Perthes had been fooled by his workmen and that his enthusiasm was greater than his common sense. On a few occasions he had indeed been fooled, for one man had been discovered at his cottage door striking flints which later he was going to 'find' in a river-bed!

The Academy of Arts and Sciences in Paris, to whom a copy of the book had been sent, appointed a commission to look into de Perthes's theories. Like many commissions, this turned out to be an excuse for doing nothing at all. For though de Perthes waited impatiently for a year for the members to turn up at Abbeville, nobody appeared. The desperate author then wrote to the members, pleading with them to see his museum and investigate his claims, and at last two worthy gentlemen did condescend to visit him.

They stayed longer than they had intended, and when they went away their faces were thoughtful and their minds disturbed.

'Yes,' they were forced to admit to their host, 'these things were made by man. You are right.'

'I know I am right!' de Perthes cried excitedly. 'Then you will tell the authorities in Paris?'

'Well—' The two men hedged. 'It would cause a very embarrassing situation. A great many people would be upset—both science and religion would be gravely affected . . .'

They returned to Paris and kept their new knowledge to themselves.

De Perthes looked gloomily at the exhibits in his museum, neatly laid out and ticketed, each with a sample of the earth in which it had been found.

'Some day the world will believe me,' he muttered.

There were several years still to pass before an important convert was made. In 1854 Dr Rigollot of Amiens, a physician and naturalist, was dragged unwillingly by a friend into de Perthes's museum. He went to scoff but remained, if not to pray, to look first with amazement, and then with wonder, at the exhibits. Finally he declared himself a fervent believer in the antiquity of man.

Dr Rigollot, fired with his new enthusiasm, began to explore the gravel deposits of the River Somme, and found hundreds of flints which had been chipped and shaped by human hands. He wrote a pamphlet about his finds; de Perthes wrote another book about his. Both were scornfully attacked.

'If these tools were made by early man,' was the new approach, 'where are the bones of these men?' Like doubting Thomas, the scoffers wanted to touch before they would believe.

'Be patient,' was the only answer that de Perthes could give, and he went on digging.

In 1859 Dr Hugh Falconer, the Vice-President of the Geological Society of London and an expert on prehistoric animals, paid a visit to the museum. He had read de Perthes's book with interest but he had not been convinced by its arguments. But when he had spent a whole day in the museum he changed his attitude as completely as Dr Rigollot had done years before.

Dr Falconer wrote immediately to his friend Joseph Prestwich, a famous geologist, and strongly advised him to go to Abbeville and see the wonderful collection.

'I am sure you will be richly rewarded,' he said.

Prestwich *was* rewarded. A few months afterwards, in company with John Evans, a young archaeologist, he arrived in Abbeville, and they too saw for themselves the evidence that man's beginnings stretched back mistily in time far beyond 4004 B.C. The two Englishmen went flint-hunting in the Somme valley—and found some!

In an address Prestwich later gave to the Royal Society he astounded his audience by declaring that the theory that man did not exist until after all the prehistoric animals had become extinct must be thrown overboard for good and all.

He held up a handful of flints.

14

'Here is the proof,' he said. 'Here are the instruments, worked by the hands of man, discovered in the depths of the globe!'

A few days later John Evans spoke to the Society of Antiquaries in similar terms. He also reminded them of the letter that John Frere had written to the secretary *sixty years* before, describing his own finds at Hoxne in Suffolk— weapons and tools which were just like those in the museum at Abbeville—and how that letter had been quietly filed and forgotten.

A note of slightly off-beat comedy now enters the story. Boucher de Perthes, heartened by the support he had received from England, set out to look for the remains of the men who had chipped the flints, convinced that it was only a question of time before they would turn up. He offered his workmen two hundred francs for the first fossil bones they brought to him.

What he might have expected would happen did happen in 1863. A workman showed him two flint hand-axes and a human tooth which he had found buried in a gravel-pit at Moulin-Quignon. The next day another tooth appeared, then a complete jawbone and another axe. De Perthes was almost speechless with excitement. Here was fossil man at last! Now let his enemies sneer. His theory was finally proved.

All his friends congratulated him. The newspapers reported the finds and visitors flocked to the scene. Members of the British Royal Society crossed the Channel to see for themselves. A French Professor of Anthropology accepted the jawbone as genuine, and de Perthes began to think that all his troubles were at an end.

Strangely, it was in England, where he had first found people to support him, that the murmurings began. They were led by Prestwich, Falconer and Evans, the very men who had stood up for him. All three happened to be in France when the sensational discovery was made.

Prestwich and Evans hurried off to Abbeville as soon as

15

they could. After examining the axes, in which they showed more interest than they did in the jaw, they reluctantly came to the conclusion that they were not prehistoric at all, but were of recent manufacture and had been made to look old. They went away without mentioning their suspicions to de Perthes.

The following day Falconer took their place. Enthusiastically, he began to dig in the pit, and was rewarded by the appearance of several more axes. He was too excited to examine them closely, and rashly declared that the jawbone must be genuine too. He changed his mind after he had returned to England and showed the flints to his colleagues.

Arguments flew across the Channel and back. The newspapers joined the battle, and harsh words were uttered in lecture rooms. There was a combined meeting of English and French scholars in the Museum of Natural History in Paris, but no agreement was reached.

The man who stood out most obstinately against the French was John Evans, who had himself bought a forged tool from an Abbeville workman for five francs. He persuaded de Perthes to accept yet another visitor to the site, and sent Mr H. Keeting, an expert cave excavator, to watch the men at work and do his own digging when they had gone.

After eight days of detective work Keeting made his report. In it he said that there was no doubt that de Perthes had been swindled by workmen who were out for the two hundred francs. The jawbone and the axes found near it were false. The jawbone was certainly old, but not prehistoric. The axes were modern . . .

That was that. The archaeologists accepted the verdict, some with relief, many with disappointment. Nobody cast any blame on the luckless de Perthes. He had been the too-trusting victim of his greedy and unscrupulous helpers. Though afterwards he always refused to admit that the jawbone was not a genuine fossil, he had to be content with knowing that the long years he had spent in his researches

16

had established the early existence of man. His fellow archaeologists gave him full credit for that success, but they refused to go any further.

Boucher de Perthes died in 1868, at the age of eighty. His career had been a stormy one, but we owe to him the beginnings of the science of prehistory and the debunking of the myth that life began according to the calculations of Archbishop Ussher. The strangest strand of this complicated story is that, while the bitter arguments about de Perthes's fossil man were raging, a genuine fossil skull *had* been found . . .

CHAPTER TWO

MEN BEFORE MAN

JOACHIM NEANDER, a young priest of Düsseldorf on the River Rhine, who died in 1680, would no doubt have been very gratified to know that his name would be famous nearly three hundred years after his death. 'The people of Germany will still be singing some of the seventy hymns I composed while walking between the high limestone cliffs in the valley of the Düssel stream,' he might have said.

His *Bundeslieder* and *Dankpsalmen* are indeed still heard occasionally in churches, but the young man's pleasure would have turned to horror if he had known that it was not his spiritual songs by which he would be remembered, but because his favourite *tal*, or valley—called *Neanderthal* by the people of Düsseldorf in his honour—was the scene of the discovery of a skeleton!

'I gave them hymns,' we can hear Neander say in disgust, 'and they remember me by a heap of bones!'

In 1856 some quarry workers were clearing out a cliff cave situated sixty feet above the winding Düssel stream and a hundred feet from the top when they unearthed a skeleton. Unaware of its great age and value, they fooled around with it for a time, kicking and throwing the pieces to one another.

When they decided to get back to work, many of the

18

bones had disappeared over the twenty-feet-wide ledge on which they were standing. Only parts of the skull, the thighbones, a few ribs and a piece of the pelvis were left. The foreman gathered up the remains and took them away.

The ill-treated bones eventually came into the possession of a schoolmaster called Fühlrott, who showed them to Professor Schaafhausen of Bonn.

'Very old,' the professor decided. 'This skull belonged to a member of some barbarous and savage race.' He wrote a detailed description of it in a German scientific review.

In 1861 his article was translated and published in English. It was as if a match had been applied to a bonfire, the flames of which burned fiercely for the next ten years. Boucher de Perthes had already made his famous discoveries, and Charles Darwin had published his controversial book outlining his theory of evolution. Both events provided ammunition for and against the professor's statement. Some experts believed that the Neanderthal skull was part of the remains of an early ancestor of man; others thought that there was nothing special about it at all.

A German named Virchow went as far as to say that it was not old, only diseased. An Englishman, Dr Gibb, even diagnosed the disease—he called it hypertrophic osteitis! English scientists did not come out of the argument very well: another was convinced that the skull had belonged to an idiot with rickets. A French anthropologist answered him, perhaps with tongue in cheek, by saying that in his opinion it closely resembled that of a modern Irishman of low mentality! But Professor Mayer of Germany was not satisfied with any of these suggestions. He decided that it had belonged to a Russian Cossack killed during the campaign against Napoleon in 1814.

Such were the opinions of some of the specialists in anthropology, pathology and anatomy. There were others, fortunately, who remained calm amid the flames. Dr William King, an English anatomist, said quietly but firmly that a real ancestor of the human species had been discovered, and

19

even gave him the name by which he is still known—*Homo neanderthalensis*. (That was when poor Joachim Neander first started to turn in his grave.)

Thomas Huxley, a follower of Darwin, confirmed Dr King's opinion, adding that the skull was of a more primitive species than the ancestor of modern man. At one time he wrote of it as though it were the 'Missing Link', that much-talked-of intermediary between ape and man. It was evident that the man of the Neander Valley had possessed a very low forehead, heavy ridges over the eyes and a protruding jaw; but without the whole skeleton it was rash to make statements which might not stand up to argument.

During the years that followed the first excitement, parts of other skeletons of the same period were found in Belgian caves; but the real evidence that settled the problem was dug up by three French priests in 1908, when they were exploring a small cave, filled with dirt and fallen rock, outside the village of La-Chapelle-aux-Saints in southern France. They found flint tools and animal bones in the compressed earth that formed a false floor, but it was not until they had reached the bottom of the cavern that a filled-in ditch revealed an almost complete skeleton. They had found the oldest known burial in the world.

The skeleton was on its back, its left arm stretched out, the right one bent. Worked flints and animal bones lay all around it. The priests decided, after a brief examination, that this marvellous relic must be studied by experts. It was sent to the National Museum of Natural History in Paris, where Marcellin Boule spent several years working on it before he felt able to publish his findings. These included some very misleading ideas about the physical appearance of Neanderthal Man which have persisted right up to the present day. The reconstructed skeleton can be seen in the *Musée de l'Homme* in Paris.

Today there are more than sixty specimens of Neanderthal Man, some of which have been found in the last fifteen years. In 1950 a number of actual footprints were discovered

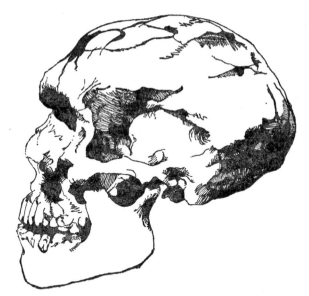

Skull of Neanderthal Man. Below, skull of modern man

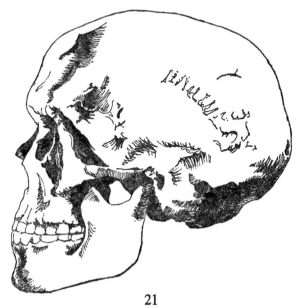

in the clayey floor of a bear-cave in the Ligurian Alps in Italy. Bones and parts of skeletons have come from France, Germany, Belgium, Italy and Spain; from Palestine and the Crimea; from Rhodesia and Tangier, and from many other places in Asia and Africa. There are differences in bone structure, but they have so many features in common that they are usually classed in one or other of two groups of Neanderthal Man, 'generalized' or 'classic'.

The popular picture of Neanderthal Man, who lived from about 100,000 to between 50,000 and 30,000 years ago, is of a grotesque, ape-like creature with a bull-neck, stooped shoulders and bent knees, low in intelligence—and covered with hair. A statue erected to him high above Les Eyzies in the Vézère Valley is impressive but unkind.

The real Neanderthal Man, though short and stocky, walked as erect as any man of today. He was intelligent enough to clean and sew animal skins for clothes, and to make fine flint tools such as scrapers, knives, hand-axes, and balls of limestone which he may have used as a bolas. (This missile, which is still used in parts of South America, consists of weights joined together by a cord. One end is held in the hand while the other is thrown around the legs of the quarry, which is brought to the ground entangled in the rope.) He lived on the bank of a stream, and he protected his 'home' by a screen of bushes or a skin fastened between two trees. When conditions were favourable, as in the Third Interglacial Period, he hunted the antelope and other small game, the rhinoceros and the elephant.

With the coming of the Fourth Glacial Period life became harder, and later Neanderthalers sheltered from the cold of the tundra wastes in caves and under rock ledges, though they first had to drive out the cave-bears and cave-lions. There they huddled round their fires, cooked their food, scraped and sewed skins and fashioned their flints. The animals they now hunted were the woolly rhinoceros and the mammoth, and the floors of the caves became littered with animals' bones.

It is thought that Neanderthal Man felt the first stirrings of 'religion'. He seems to have had a vague feeling that there was a power somewhere which had to be placated. Death was not the end of everything. The broken, motionless body, torn by some wild animal, would live and breathe, eat and hunt again. So often they buried their dead in graves, and they put food offerings and tools beside the body for it to use in a future life. In some caves bear-skulls and thigh-bones, carefully arranged so that they all point in the same direction, have been found, and in others bear-skulls were piled up in what may be called stone chests. These were perhaps talismans to bring them success in hunting, or the relics of a sacrifice made in a cave-shrine.

All this is guesswork, of course. At the most we can say that such practices were possible, even likely, but unless a Neanderthal Man could tell us with his own lips how he lived and what he thought about we must go on guessing.

Guessing, too, is necessary when we try to account for the disappearance of Neanderthal Man between 30,000 and 50,000 years ago.

Neanderthalers became extinct, perhaps, because they could not adapt themselves to the worsening climatic conditions of the Fourth Glacial Period. The world was becoming colder, they could not find enough caves or rock shelters, food was more difficult to come by; and no doubt many of them died of hunger or exposure. When the peak of the glacial period had been passed their numbers must have been considerably reduced.

Meanwhile a new race of men, *real* men—tall, muscular, and of a more modern appearance—had reached Europe. Their culture was more advanced than that of Neanderthal Man, for they used ivory and bone as well as stone for tools, and they painted on cave walls. The Neanderthalers could not stand the competition and remained separate. Some of them were no doubt absorbed by the newcomers, but the world now belonged to *Homo sapiens,* the ancestors of us all.

CHAPTER THREE

THE PAINTED CAVE

IN the cloudless blue sky over the English Channel and the coast of Kent, British and German planes were shooting each other down in one of the most vital battles of the Second World War. At the same time on the ground, in the Dordogne district of southern France, five youths, the eldest seventeen years old, were out shooting rabbits. Both sides made exaggerated claims about their successes in the air battle, but the result of the ground operation is not in any doubt, for it led to one of the most thrilling and valuable archaeological discoveries that has ever been made.

Ravidat, Marsal and Queroy lived in the small country town of Montignac. Coencas and Estreguil were refugees, and refugees, strange to say, in their own country. In that unhappy period, in September 1940, part of France was occupied by the Germans, and there were many people who had managed to escape into the unoccupied part. With the five youths on their rabbiting expedition was Robot, a mongrel dog belonging to Ravidat, and one of the most famous dogs in history!

About twenty minutes' walk southwards from Montignac is a limestone ridge, sparsely dotted with pine trees, called Lascaux. During a storm which took place about twenty years before the story begins a tree had been uprooted and

24

had left a gaping hole in the ground. An unfortunate donkey had stumbled into the hole, had broken its legs and died before being found. Its bones were still lying round the hole, which was now nearly hidden by overgrown scrub, when the five boys passed by, their minds fixed on only one thing—a rabbit for the stewpot.

Suddenly Ravidat noticed that Robot was no longer with them. He called and whistled, but no small scruffy dog bounded up with wagging tail. They searched the hillside, and at last heard barking. It sounded muffled, as though it were coming from under their feet, below the ground!

The puzzled boys eventually found the hole among a tumbled mass of stones and the donkey's whitened bones. Ravidat decided that he must try to rescue the dog. Using knife, sticks and bare hands, they cut the weeds and scrub away, and tugged at the stones until the gap was wide enough for Ravidat to slither through. Hesitantly he edged his way down a slope, the uncertain light from his torch, which was not working well, hardly helping him at all. Wondering all the time what was going to happen next, he suddenly lost his balance and fell!

He landed up on the sandy floor of a cave twenty-five feet below the surface of the ground, bruised and shaken, but all in one piece. Above him he could just see a sliver of daylight, almost blotted out by the heads of his friends as they peered over the edge of the hole. From near his feet there came a whimpering bark—Robot!

Ravidat had had the presence of mind to keep a grip on his torch. He switched it on and bent to stroke his beloved mongrel, now looking scruffier than ever. When he had made sure that Robot had broken no bones, he began to take stock of his surroundings. There were rocky walls around him. He was in a good-sized cave passage. He wondered how far it extended under the hill. Exploring it would be good fun—even better than rabbiting!

Ravidat called his friends, and the four boys slid down to join him. They all had matches with them. Eking them

25

out carefully, they made their way further into the gloom, with Robot reluctantly bringing up the rear. Soon the passage widened into a great cavern, thirty feet across, and the roof was far above the trembling yellow light thrown by their matches and the dying torch. They noticed that the face of the rock was twisted and folded as though clouds had been turned into stone in a rocky sky.

They gazed about them, fearful yet excited, and awed by the immensity, the darkness and the silence. Suddenly Ravidat gave a shout.

'Look! Look over there! Horses!'

The others swivelled round. Horses? In an underground cave? What nonsense was Ravidat talking?

But there *were* horses, painted on the cave walls and on the roof; and other animals too, some recognizable as antlered stags and enormous bulls. And, what was more, they all seemed to be moving; some slowly and purposefully, others as though they would at any moment leap off the wall and charge the astonished boys.

As their eyes took in the staggering sight they saw that they were surrounded by animals; yellow, brown and red ones, others just black outlines. Some were drawn on top of others. It was like visiting a picture gallery in a nightmare. Heedless of everything but the fantastic display, the boys struck match after match, until the last one flickered out and they had to grope their way back to the entrance, scrabble up the steep slope and reach the outside world.

They walked back to Montignac, saying little, their minds still aflame with wonder. Before they parted they decided not to tell anybody about their find, but to meet the following day to explore the cave more methodically. Even Robot was sworn to secrecy!

Every day for the next five days they returned to their secret rendezvous, taking torches and ropes with them, and explored more of the unknown interior. The first chamber, they discovered, had two narrower galleries opening from it, the right-hand one splitting again into right and left

Reindeer and bulls painted on the cave walls at Lascaux

forks. At the end of the right fork there was a straight-sided pit thirty feet deep.

Everywhere there were animals. In the main hall were six huge bulls, four of them complete, the largest about sixteen feet long. Underneath the black outlines, spotted with black, were fainter, older paintings, dark red in colour. One strange creature, also in the main hall, puzzled the boys a great deal. It had the body of a rhinoceros, but its head was like that of an antelope with two enormous horns. Some little black horses ran round the flat of the wall. A cow seemed to be jumping over them. In the left hand passage they saw another cow, a black bull and a horse falling upside down. In the right-hand passage there were goats' heads, bison, and a fifteen-feet-long frieze of swimming deer.

There must have been hundreds of pictures, some vivid, some blurred—animals standing alone, in groups, and painted one on top of another. There were also masses of engravings which were difficult to identify because they were so inextricably mixed up. Several geometrically shaped objects were perhaps meant to represent traps.

The boys were astonished at the marvellous state of preservation of the pictures. The colours were so clean and brilliant that many of them looked as if they had only been painted a short time before. This, they were told afterwards, was because the cave had not been affected by frost or extreme changes of temperature. It had known neither summer nor winter. A thin hard film of calcite crystals which covered some of the paintings had also acted as a preserving varnish and had made them shine like glass. Other pictures had been painted over the crystal screen.

At the end of the week the five boys knew that it would be impossible to keep the secret to themselves. It could no longer be 'their' cave. Ravidat knew a little about prehistoric things and realized that they had stumbled across something of tremendous importance to archaeologists.

They decided to tell the local schoolmaster, M. Leon Laval, who had once taken a party of boys to see some similar caves. They were not altogether surprised when M. Laval put on a 'You're pulling my leg' expression when he had heard the incoherent account of the fantastic things they had seen, but they were relieved when he agreed to accompany them to the cave.

M. Laval's doubts changed to a blazing excitement when he stood in the great cavern and flashed his torch on the roof and walls. He shook his head, drew in his breath and whispered, 'But this is incredible—who would have believed all this was here? Right under our feet . . .'

When they were standing again on the hillside they held a conference. That is, M. Laval talked, and the boys listened.

'First of all,' he declared, 'we must inform the Comte and Comtesse de Rochefoucauld, who own the land round here. Then someone who knows more about prehistoric art than any man living *must* come and see the paintings.'

'Who is that?' Ravidat asked.

'The Abbé Breuil,' M. Laval replied in a tone full of awe. 'He is staying at Brive, only twenty miles away. I know M. Thaon, a friend of his. He will see that the Abbé comes . . .'

So, nine days after Robot had started the whole thing, the famous French archaeologist confirmed that the boys had discovered the most magnificent paintings of the Upper Palaeolithic Age ever found in France, perhaps even in Europe.

The Abbé Breuil spent a lot of time in the cave, studying and copying the pictures. News of the discovery spread over the district, and even though it was wartime and petrol was rationed there was a stream of visitors. They were not allowed to climb down into the cavern, but the Abbé would talk to them in the open when, every so often, he emerged from the entrance hole, blinking his eyes like a mole in daylight.

In October 1940 the Abbé presented his first report on his work in the cave. Then a silence descended on Lascaux, as far as the outside world was concerned, though experts were busy with their records and photographs.

After the war a department of the French Government took over and arranged for the cave to be opened to the public. A new entrance was excavated, and two thick doors were built to guard the main hall. Electric light was installed, the lamps shining from the floor upwards, and guides were appointed to show visitors round. Two of them were none other than two of the five boys who are the heroes of this story—Ravidat and Marsal, who were by that time growing into men.

There is one part of the cave that visitors did not see—the pit at the end of the right-hand fork. Only privileged people were allowed to descend by rope ladder. Right at the bottom, on a projection of the wall surface, is an extraordinary picture—a Stone Age story!

A bison has been wounded, perhaps by a woolly rhinoceros that seems to be ambling away from the scene. The bison's entrails are spilling on to the ground. A cartoon man, drawn with a young child's crudeness, with a head more bird-like than human, and with four fingers on each hand, is lying in front of the bison's lowered head. By his side is a stick surmounted by a bird, and near his feet is a spear-thrower.

What is the meaning of this strange scene? Was the artist describing an incident that had taken place somewhere outside the cave all those thousands of years ago? Had the hunter been killed by the bison before that animal was attacked by the rhinoceros? Or had the hunter killed the bison and had himself broken his neck in the fight? Why has he got a bird head? Is the stick a totem pole, or is the bird the soul of the man escaping after death? Perhaps the man is not dead, but in a trance . . . The Abbé Breuil thought that the hunter might be buried in the floor under the picture, but excavations revealed nothing but stones and some charcoal.

The question that still puzzles archaeologists about all

the many caves that contain Stone Age paintings is: why? Why did the artists choose the most inaccessible parts of the deepest caves and, with the aid of crude lamps, perhaps made of a wick of twisted moss floating in a limestone saucer filled with fat, lavish their skill on rock faces difficult to reach and hidden in blackness?

We can only guess the answer, of course, but most people think that the paintings and engravings were connected with sorcery and magical rites, and that the caves were meeting places in which these Old Stone Age men held their ceremonies.

Life in those times was hard, brutal and short, and death came in many different and fearful ways. In winter people were cold and food was scarce. Their main occupation was hunting. A plentiful supply of animals was necessary if life was to go on; and if the animals would not appear of their own accord, then they had to be persuaded to—by magic.

So the magicians of the tribe drew the animals they wanted to hunt, and they drew them with spears and harpoons sticking out of their bodies. They drew them dying, and they drew them heavy with young, so that there would always be new, live animals to follow the old, dead ones. These secret, symbolic hunting grounds represented the kind of hunting they wanted in the world above. They lived out their needs and desires by a kind of play-acting, just as primitive hunting races such as the Australian aborigines do today.

It is likely that the artist-magician, dressed like an animal, would lead a magic hunting dance before throwing spears at the painted symbols as a prelude to a real hunt, in which lives would be risked and perhaps lost.

Magic and religion apart, the paintings of Lascaux and of similar caves show a great feeling for form and design, and a desire to create beauty for its own sake. The artists knew how to use their materials. They were not daunted by the difficulties of perspective, and they used the natural curves and crevices of the rocks to achieve depth and realism. We

B

do not know exactly what they used to paint with—possibly feathers or animal hair fixed into small bones, and also hollow bones through which the colours were squirted on to a surface prepared with fat and oil in order to produce a cloudy texture. Reds and yellows were obtained from natural ochres and animal fats, pounded into powder. Black came from manganese dioxide and charcoal.

The story ends on a sombre note, for something of a tragedy has happened at Lascaux. During the years since the cave was opened to the public the pictures have been gradually fading, the colours losing their brilliance. A green micro-organism is spreading over some of them, and even the great bull's dignity has been lessened by this creeping fungus.

In the spring of 1963 Lascaux was closed, and a committee of scientists was appointed by the French Government to try to deal with the problem. Whether the condition is due to the air-conditioning plant installed in 1952 or to the breath exhaled by the thousands of visitors is not yet established. When the last sightseer had gone the paintings were photographed and the entrance sealed. Scientific instruments, controlled from outside, are recording what is happening inside, measuring the rate of the growth of the spreading fungus and the extent of the crumbling of the rock walls into powder.

It would be a sad thing if the wonderful paintings of Lascaux could never again be seen, but if the alternative is their slow but steady disintegration, then the price, though heavy, would be worth while. We shall always have the memory of the pleasure, excitement and awe they have given to archaeologists and to the general public for nearly a quarter of a century.

CHAPTER FOUR

VILLAGE ON STILTS

THE winter of 1853 was one of the coldest the Swiss people had ever known. There was not much snow, but the temperature remained arctic for weeks on end. The level of the water in rivers and lakes fell lower than anybody had ever seen it, and not even the oldest inhabitants could remember when there had been such a time.

Lake Zurich looked more like a large puddle than a lake. Its edges, usually lapped by clear water, were now stony beaches, and even when spring came there was no relief from the strange drought. The snow, which on melting normally kept the lakes provided with water, still covered the mountains and looked as though it was going to be a permanent fixture.

Though the Swiss had to endure many hardships during this time, they were quick to take advantage of the newly exposed land left by the retreating waters. They built walls of earth and stone from the old shore line out to the new one, and filled the space in between with mud they dredged from the shallow lake water. Thus a new field was formed—for fields were scarce in that mountainous area—and the lake had a permanent new shore line.

The village of Obermeilen lay on the north side of the lake, about six miles from the town of Zurich. The enterprising villagers started to make their new fields by building the enclosing walls. Then they began to dredge up the mud from beyond them. They had not got very far, however, when they came upon unexpected obstacles.

Just below the surface they found the tops of long thick wooden posts which had evidently been sunk into the bottom of the mud. Some of the posts were up to twelve feet long, and they had been planted about a foot apart.

The puzzled workmen tried again, further out, and then again, but always they came up against this forest of piles. In the end they found that a four-hundred-yards stretch of the bay was so covered, and that the piles began about a hundred yards from the shore and stretched inwards towards the middle of the lake.

No new fields, thought the disgruntled villagers. They were not pacified when all sorts of strange objects came up out of the dredged mud. There were bones, pieces of flint and wood, bronze axes and bracelets. One of the farmers suggested that it was time they tried to solve the mystery, so he and some of his friends went to see the wisest man in Obermeilen, taking with them some of the finds.

The wisest man was the village schoolmaster, and he soon realized that the farmers had stumbled across something that might be very important from an archaeological point of view. He could not explain what the discovery meant himself, but he knew who could. But first he spent several days groping in the mud with the dredgers, and the result was another pile of antlers, knives and axes. By this time the workmen were being very careful, and everything that seemed to be of human workmanship was handled as reverently as though it were made of gold. Then the schoolmaster returned home and wrote a letter to Professor Ferdinand Keller, the President of the Zurich Antiquarian Society. In it he declared that in his opinion the lake-bed had uncovered man-made relics which might throw light on the earliest inhabitants of Switzerland.

Professor Keller got together a working party which went

to Obermeilen, and dredging was resumed vigorously. It was impossible to 'dig' in the usual way or to make accurate recordings of the finds because they were buried in the soft peaty mud below the low-lying water. Some of the investigators took to boats. They twisted and turned over the heads of the piles, and they used grabs to pick up any object they could detect on the lake bottom. Others scrabbled among the stuff that the villagers had already taken out of the lake, searching for what might be hidden in it.

This went on until the beginning of the summer in 1854. Then the snow on the mountains really did begin to melt, and the water trickled down into the lake and caused the level to rise almost to its usual height. The excavations came to an end, and the finds were taken to Zurich and examined by experts.

The bronze axes were found to be of two kinds—flat ones with flanges on the sides, and heavier ones with a hole for the shaft. There was a great variety of flint tools, including axes, chisels and knives. The latter were set in wooden grips, and this surprised Professor Keller very much, for wood of a very great age is not usually preserved. Then he realized that water could prevent the decay of materials which exposure to the air would normally cause. He was even more surprised when cleaning revealed bits of basketwork, and fragments of cloth and netting. This was the first time that such things had been recovered in recognizable form. A remarkable find indeed! Thousands of bones were among the objects, and these were identified as those of foxes, goats, pigs, cows, sheep, dogs and deer.

The piles sticking up in the water had not been neglected, either. It was found that they were in more or less straight rows; some of them had cross-beams connecting them, and there was even evidence of the wooden floors that had been laid on the beams. The whole thing had been a village built by people of the New Stone Age . . .

In 1858 another submerged lake village was excavated. This one was at Robenhausen, about twenty miles from

35

Swiss lake village.

Zurich, near a little lake called Pfäffikon, a natural reservoir, with only the River Aa as outlet.

There was a thick layer of peat at the foot of the lake-end over which the Aa flowed on its way out. The course of the river was being straightened and deepened so that a spinning-mill could be supplied with water, and during the digging the workmen came across some wooden piles in the peat-bed. It was not to the village schoolmaster they went this time to report their find, but to a farm labourer.

This was Jakob Messikommer, twenty-nine years old, intelligent, imaginative, and a glutton for knowledge of all kinds. The men knew that he would be interested in their information and would know what to do about it. Messikommer did—he reported the discovery immediately to Professor Keller. Then he gave all the time he could spare to helping the diggers and collecting whatever turned up.

Although he had a large family to support, Messikommer's passion for archaeology was so intense that he decided to give up farm work and devote the rest of his life to exploring the remains of the village that had been under water for thousands of years. He managed to buy the land on either side of the site, a piece at a time, and for more than fifty years he continued digging, one small section after another.

He used a hand pump and wooden buckets to drain the water away, working patiently and methodically, and his techniques improved greatly with experience. The top level of soil, which never contained anything interesting, was first removed from a patch about twenty square yards in area. Then, when the tops of the piles were exposed, every spadeful of earth was examined closely for potsherds, stone tools, worked bones, knives, daggers, wooden cups, and anything else which might turn up.

Over the years, as the work progressed, it was possible to form a detailed picture of the lives and times of the Neolithic people who had lived in that part of the world. Scale models of lake villages were displayed in museums. The villages,

37

it was seen, had been built on platforms stretching in long lines above the mud of the shore and had been supported by piles. At one time it was thought that the villages had actually been built over the water. Then it was realized that the level of lakes had risen considerably since Neolithic times and had eventually covered the mud foundations of the villages.

Some lake villages grew to be quite large. In one of them fifty thousand posts had held it above ground level. The inhabitants seem to have been very prosperous. Their houses contained wooden furniture, and they used pitchers, spoons, dishes, bowls, jars and kettles. Their tools were ground-edged, and included chisels mounted in deer-horn handles, flint knives with wooden handles, harpoons of antler, arrowheads of flint, and awls and needles of bone. They wove linen from flax, and made fishing-nets, ropes, matting, wickerwork baskets and raffia mats; and they ate apples and hazel-nuts as well as animal flesh and grain such as wheat and barley.

That all these things were preserved was due to the slightly acid water of the lake; in ordinary circumstances they would have perished. Thus we have scraps of the earliest cloth that has ever been found in western Europe, and wooden articles that have never before been found so complete.

So it was that a freezing winter that brought misery and hardship to most people enabled Professor Keller, with help later from Jakob Messikommer, to reconstruct a little-known aspect of his country's past, and brought the vanished world of pile-built villages into the pattern of prehistory.

CHAPTER FIVE

THE ROYAL GRAVES OF UR

ONE of the most outstanding excavators of this century was Sir Leonard Woolley, who died in 1960 at the age of seventy-nine. He was also a man of imagination, a writer of great distinction, and one of the nicest people in the world of archaeology.

Though all Woolley's work was important and dramatic, what appealed most to the public imagination was the discovery of the Royal Graves of Ur.

Up to the middle of the nineteenth century archaeology in Mesopotamia, the bleak desert land between the two rivers Tigris and Euphrates, was concerned with the Assyrians and Babylonians, about whom much was known, both from Bible stories and from the writers of the ancient world.

No one had heard of the Sumerians, for they had been forgotten even by the time of Alexander the Great. Today, thanks to people like Sir Leonard Woolley, we know that astronomy, mathematics, the calendar, agriculture, architecture, government and law and, above all, writing, all had their beginnings in Sumer.

Between 1850 and 1900 scraps of evidence about these mysterious people were mounting up, chiefly through the thousands of clay tablets inscribed with cuneiform writing, cylinder seals and statues that from time to time were picked up. During the investigation of a tall mound in 1854, tablets were found which identified the site as that of Ur. But it was Woolley who finally unlocked the treasure chest of the lost civilization and revealed its secrets.

Sumerian bas-relief

The expedition of which he was the Director was sponsored jointly by the British Museum and the University Museum of Pennsylvania. For ten of the twelve seasons Leonard Woolley (he had not then been knighted) had his wife as one of his assistants, for six years Professor Mallowan, famous for his archaeological work in Mesopotamia, and many other experienced people. To all of them Woolley has paid generous tribute for their team work.

Before they started, in 1922, Ur was nothing but a number of sand-covered mounds between Baghdad and the Persian Gulf. Five thousand years ago it was a busy port, but the head of the Persian Gulf had retreated seventy or so miles to the south. The first excavations brought to light parts of the wall which had surrounded the city, and just outside it a huge rubbish dump, forty feet thick. The layers of debris showed that the citizens of Ur had been throwing their refuse over the wall for about four thousand years! There were bones, broken clay pots, household refuse and clay tablets.

Deep shafts were dug into the rubbish, and a cemetery of more than 1,400 graves was found and thoroughly explored between 1929 and 1930. The burials had been simple ones, with coffins of wood, clay or basket work, and some skeletons were wrapped only in matting. The graves which were nearest the surface had been robbed of their contents, but others contained pots, jugs, tools, trinkets and other things that the dead person had valued in life.

The grave robbers had dug shafts and made tunnels in their well-planned efforts to get rich quickly, and at the bottom of one of the shafts Woolley found a hoard of copper weapons and a dagger with a golden blade and a hilt of lapis lazuli in a sheath of gold, perhaps dropped or overlooked by the thieves. Next to it was a set of toilet instruments, also of gold. Nothing like this had ever before been found in Mesopotamia. The excavators were tense with expectancy. What would they find next? . . .

The next thing, as it turned out, could not be called treasure. In another part of the cemetery they found a floor, made of limestone slabs, which lay at the bottom of a large pit. The surprising thing about this was that there was none of this type of stone in the Euphrates Valley. The houses of Sumer had been built of mud bricks. It must have been brought from a quarry at least thirty miles away, and it was unlikely that it had been transported all that distance just to make an underground pavement. Here was a mystery indeed. But before it could be solved the digging had to stop. The hot season had arrived, and nothing more could be done until the autumn.

During the summer Woolley decided that perhaps the slabs were not part of a floor, but the roof of an underground building. They were on the verge, it might be, of discovering the grave of a Sumerian king! The summer could not pass quickly enough.

There was indeed a tomb but, apart from a few pieces of a gold diadem and some corroded copper pots, it was empty. Grave robbers had been there first, and they had made a tunnel, now rubbish-filled, from the roof to the floor of the empty grave.

During the 1928–29 season two more large tombs were discovered. They consisted of a four-roomed building at the bottom of a shaft. The walls and roofs were of limestone, the two larger rooms were vaulted and the two smaller ones in the centre were crowned with domes. There was an arched door in the outer wall, approached by a ramp, and the doors between the rooms were arched too. Both tombs, alas, were empty.

More disappointment, balanced by determination to carry on. Surely, thought the excavators, success could not be far away.

It was not, though no one foresaw just what a tremendous success it was going to be. It happened in another part of the cemetery. There was a shallow sloping trench, and in it five bodies were lying side by side, copper daggers at their waists.

This was an unusual sort of burial—five people buried together with none of the grave-goods that one would expect. The skeletons were photographed and carefully removed, and it was found that they had been lying on a bed of matting. More of the matting was exposed when the sand and rubbish was brushed away. Further down the slope, at the bottom of a pit, there was another group of skeletons, women's this time, in two rows of five. They wore headdresses of gold, blue lapis lazuli and pink cornelian, and strings of beads round their necks—but again there were no tomb furnishings.

42

Just past the bodies were the remains of a harp of magnificent workmanship and beautifully decorated, with gold-capped nails and the sounding-box edged with a mosaic in red, white and blue stones. On the front of the box was the golden head of a bull. The wood was decayed but the decoration was intact, so that the whole instrument could be reconstructed. The bones of the harpist lay across it.

The next discovery was made further along the pit—animal bones and what had been a wooden chariot, mounted on runners like a sledge, also decorated with gold, lapis lazuli and shell. There were gold and silver heads of lions and bulls on the side panels and along the top rail. The bones belonged to the asses that had pulled the chariot and to their grooms who lay by their heads.

The pit was crowded with precious things. The excavators were delighted and bewildered. They took out of the dust and rubble an inlaid gaming board, tools and weapons of silver, gold, alabaster, marble and lapis lazuli; bowls and copper vessels, and a golden drinking tube. They uncovered more human bones. Then came the wreckage of a wooden chest, about six feet long and three feet wide, which may have held clothes. It was empty now, but behind it were so many more wonderful things that it was like being in Aladdin's cave. They included a set of silver vessels and tall, slender tumblers, a goblet, a plain oval bowl of gold and two lions' heads of silver.

But where was the person who had owned all these treasures? Among the skeletons there had not been one of a more obviously exalted position than the rest. All that had been found so far was a preliminary—but to what?

The objects were taken out of the pit slowly and carefully, until only the chest remained. When that was moved another surprise awaited the team. Underneath it was the roof of another tomb! In the roof was a hole over which the chest had been placed, deliberately, it seemed, to hide the fact that the tomb had been entered by people who had no right to be there. Like so many of the other graves, this one had also been plundered.

Was this, then, the end of the search? No, for when they had dug around the new tomb they found another ramp leading to another pit like the one six feet above. At the foot of the ramp they uncovered the skeletons of six soldiers with copper helmets and spears. Just inside the pit were the remains of two four-wheeled ox-drawn wagons, though only an impression of the decayed wood was left in the soil. The bones of six oxen, the grooms and the drivers were there too.

Next, against the end wall of the chamber, leaned nine skeletons. They had been women wearing elaborate head-dresses with pendants shaped like beech leaves, great golden moon-shaped ear-rings, silver hair ornaments, and necklaces of lapis lazuli and gold. The space between the women and the wagons was crowded with more skeletons, both men and women; and a passage along the edge of the tomb was lined with soldiers. There were two more harps, one on top of the women against the wall, and another by the side wall of the pit.

There was enough evidence in the plundered tomb to show that it had contained several bodies, one of them an important person. The inscription on a cylinder seal suggests that his name was A-bar-gi. The robbers had overlooked two model boats. One, of silver, was very well preserved, with stern and prow, oars, five seats, and an arch for an awning to protect the passenger from the sun. Boats of the same type are still in use on the Lower Euphrates.

Behind the end of A-bar-gi's empty tomb-chamber there was another one, with a vaulted brick roof. The weight of earth above it had caused it to cave in, but when the debris was removed it was clear that no robbers had entered.

For here was the climax of the search, worth all the disappointments and false starts. Here was the tomb of a lady of quality, to whom the upper pit, with its sledge-chariot, had belonged. Even her name was there—Shub-ad, engraved on a cylinder seal found in the shaft above the chamber roof.

Shub-ad lay on the remains of a wooden bier. The upper part of her body was covered with beads of gold, silver and semi-precious stones; a great collar of them reached to her waist. Her headdress was an elaborate creation of ribbons, flowers, beech and willow leaves, all of gold, the flower petals inlaid with blue and white. It had been fixed to a wig, at the back of which had been a golden comb. Rings hung from her ears to her shoulders. The various parts of the headdress lay in such good order that, later on, Woolley was able to reconstruct it on a wax head that Mrs Woolley modelled.

Near the lady's hand was a gold cup, and by her side a spare headdress made of white leather and covered with thousands of tiny blue beads.

Two women attendants, one at the foot and one at the head of the bier, were next unearthed; then came all sorts of grave-goods, silver and copper vessels, stone bowls and clay jars; and some large cockle-shells containing green paint. This, perhaps, had been used as a cosmetic for the eyelids.

That is the story of how the Royal Graves were found. But there were still many questions that had to be answered. Who were these people? When did they die? Why were they buried with such pomp and ritual?

Woolley's reconstruction of the magnificent yet horrible story is generally accepted by most scholars, though we shall probably never know the exact truth. It revealed that the people of Sumer about 2,700 B.C. held beliefs that set them apart from all other peoples living at that time, and certainly far apart from the twentieth century.

Woolley's conclusion was that the graves were those of King A-bar-gi and Queen Shub-ad, two of the rulers of Ur in its very early days, before the Kings of Ur ruled over the whole of Sumer. They may have been husband and wife. The king, Woolley thought, had died first and was buried, and before the queen died she expressed a wish to lie near her husband. So the king's shaft was re-opened by grave-diggers as far as the top of the chamber vault, then they dug down at the back of the king's tomb to make the queen's burial chamber.

It seems likely that the workmen stole the treasures of the king's grave by breaking open the brick roof, then placed the clothes chest over the hole to avert suspicion. That seems to be the only explanation for the plundered grave of the king lying immediately below the untouched grave of the queen. The excavators later found other royal graves where the vaults had been robbed by men who had tunnelled into them, but in every case the pit at the bottom of the sloping ramp had been undisturbed.

When a king or queen died it was evidently the custom for members of the court—servants, soldiers, musicians, courtiers, ladies-in-waiting, grooms and chariot-drivers—to die too. In another death-pit, the largest in the cemetery, the bodies of six men were found near a large copper basin, and sixty-eight women, each wearing a silver headband, though as streaks of purplish powder they were hardly re-cognizable, were lying in regular rows on the floor, so neatly, with nothing in disarray, that they could not have suffered a violent death. Most of the skeletons had one arm bent towards the mouth; beside each one was a cup.

One of the women had not put on her silver ribbon. Woolley found it rolled up near the body, in what had been her pocket. She had either forgotten to put it on, or she had been late for her appointment with death . . .

All these people must have entered the grave before they died, and they died peacefully and willingly after drinking a poisonous liquid that killed them in a drugged sleep, counting it an honour to accompany their king or queen into the after-life.

Then the wagons and chariots were backed down the ramp past the guard of soldiers, and the asses and oxen were killed before the grooms themselves drank the deadly poison. Before the cups were filled from the copper basin

46

there would be a solemn funeral service, with prayers and chants. And when all the people were dead someone would come and put the bodies in order. When all was as it should be, and the dead king, in his own tomb with his personal attendants, had received his last honours, the pit was filled in. Earth covered the men and women and the treasures of the royal household. Covered for ever, thought the mourners; for only five thousand years, as it turned out . . .

Some archaeologists argue against the theory that the graves were royal. They think they might have been designed for the victims of sacrifices carried out at a New Year's Day festival, for on that day the chief religious ceremony of the year was held to ensure fertility of crops, cattle, and women. If this were the case the victims were priests and priestesses, not kings and queens—mock rulers chosen just for that one occasion. But Woolley's theory is strengthened by the fact that two cylinder seals found in the ruins of Ur bore inscriptions which definitely called the owner 'king'. One of them, indeed, said, 'A-kalam-dug, King of Ur', which would seem to settle the matter.

CHAPTER SIX

QUEST FOR TROY

THE ancient Greeks were nourished on the epics of their poet Homer. His *Iliad* and *Odyssey* were their Bible, giving dramatists ideas for plays, artists ideas for sculptures and thinkers ideas to discuss.

The poems described the marvellous adventures of gods and men and furnished the Greeks with ideals of heroism, morality, religion and politics. The language of the poems is noble, elegantly simple and strikingly beautiful. The heroes are Achilles, the turbulent death-dealer, brave but ruthless; Odysseus, strong and cunning, caring little for the gods; and Hector, the noble dreamer, whose fate it was to be dragged by the heels round the walls of Troy.

It was Hector who, on the eve of battle, prophesied to his wife that proud Troy would go down in ruins, together with its king and the king's people.

When Heinrich Schliemann started his quest for Troy his aim was to give flesh and substance to Homer's legends; to prove that they were history too; and to make the three heroes, and Paris, Menelaus and the fair Helen, live again.

Heinrich Schliemann was born in 1822 at Neu-Buckow, in the German state of Mecklenberg-Schwerin. His father was the pastor of a small village called Ankershagen. The Schliemann family was always on the edge of poverty, and there were few luxuries for Heinrich and his six brothers and sisters. Yet the boy was not unhappy during his early years.

Pastor Schliemann fed his son's imagination by telling him legends, fairy tales, episodes from local history (some of which he made up on the spur of the moment!) and, above all, vivid stories of the Greek heroes which he had read in translations of Homer.

One Christmas, when Heinrich was seven, his father gave him a massive book of 'universal history'. Eagerly the boy turned the pages. Now he would be able to read for himself all about the heroes of Ancient Greece. One in particular of the many engravings took his fancy, a highly dramatic portrayal of Aeneas bearing Anchises, his aged father, on his back, and leading his son by the hand as they sought escape from burning Troy through the mighty Scaean Gate. Behind the city walls huge flames engulfed the citadel after it had been sacked by the victorious Greeks.

Heinrich gazed at the scene of tragic grandeur and thought that one day he *must* see for himself the gutted ruins of Troy. He found it impossible to believe that all traces of Troy had vanished from the face of the earth, that no one even knew for certain the exact spot where it had stood. Walls that withstood ten years of siege could *not* have been entirely crushed into dust.

'One day,' the boy cried excitedly to his father, 'I shall excavate the walls of Troy myself!' The pastor smiled tolerantly.

In 1832 Heinrich's mother died and he was sent to stay with his uncle, also a pastor, in another part of Mecklenberg, and went to school there. He became a very good Latin scholar—his Christmas present to his father that year was an essay in Latin on the Trojan War—and all his masters forecast a brilliant future for him. But when he was eleven, and had just started at the Gymnasium (a kind of grammar school), his father got into trouble with the church authorities and had to resign. Heinrich had to leave the

Gymnasium as they could no longer afford the fees, and continue at an ordinary school. He left school altogether when he was fourteen and became a grocer's assistant . . .

The shop was in Fürstenberg, a small industrial town on the River Oder. Every day he started work at 5 a.m. and did not finish until 11 p.m. He never had a moment for rest or study, but in spite of all the drudgery he never lost his love of learning. It was a flame that would not let itself be extinguished.

Fuel for the flame was provided by a young man named Hermann Niederhoffer, a parson's son who had been expelled from school and was working as a miller. One day Niederhoffer went into the grocer's shop to buy potato whisky, and drunkenly began to recite some lines of Homer in Greek. In the dimly lit shop Schliemann listened spellbound to the music of the words although he did not understand a single one of them. When he knew what he was listening to he made Niederhoffer repeat the lines again and again, and rewarded him by paying for the whisky himself. All his old yearnings about Troy had come back, and he made a fierce resolution, then and there, that he would learn Greek himself.

His servitude in the grocer's shop came to an end when he strained himself badly while trying to lift a heavy cask, and he realized that he would have to find a less strenuous job. He did not know then that the accident would change his whole life and fortunes.

Full of ambition, he set off for Hamburg, his only assets thirty Prussian dollars and a knowledge of the grocery trade. The bustling port filled him with high hopes, but they were soon shattered when the only work he could get was in another grocer's shop! Soon he was worse off than ever he had been, with no money and no prospects. He decided he must make a clean break with the past. He managed to get a job as cabin boy on the brig *Dorothea*, which was about to sail for Venezuela. He sold everything he had to buy clothes and a blanket, and on November 28,

1841, he boarded the *Dorothea*, full of fine romantic thoughts about South America.

For a few days all went well. In his few free moments Schliemann began to teach himself Spanish, and neither seasickness nor the storm that was blowing up deterred him.

Soon, however, the storm became ugly. All the signs pointed to disaster, and disaster came on the night of December 11. The storm reached its peak, the little ship gave up the struggle, and the captain gave orders to abandon ship. After plunging into the water just as the ship heeled over for the last time, Schliemann was pulled on to the only lifeboat still afloat, and he and the other survivors were tossed about mercilessly for nine hours while the storm raged around them.

The first light of day showed them that they were being blown towards the Dutch island of Texel. Soon they were thawing themselves out before a roaring farmhouse fire.

The *Dorothea* adventure marked the lowest point in Schliemann's fortunes. After getting a job in an office in Amsterdam he started seriously to study languages. He taught himself English by reading aloud, writing essays, attending the English Church and repeating the sermon word by word. Within six months he was speaking English fluently.

Eventually he took only six weeks to learn a language, and quickly added French, Italian, Portuguese and Russian to his repertoire, and then the languages of the countries with which his firm did business; Danish, Swedish, Norwegian and Polish. By the time he was thirty-four he also knew both ancient and modern Greek; two years later he had perfected his schoolboy Latin; and later still Arabic, Turkish and Persian.

Schliemann, through his business ability and his driving ambition, made his fortune. In 1863 he decided that he was rich enough to give up his business interests and spend the rest of his life doing the things he had always dreamed of doing; the chief of which was, of course, to fulfil the vow he had made when he was seven—to find Homer's Troy . . .

Most historians and scholars considered that Schliemann was nothing but a wealthy eccentric who had condemned himself to a wild-goose chase. They believed that Troy had only existed in legend. The few who thought that the story might have a basis in truth had decided that a mound at the village of Bounarbashi, about nine miles from the Aegean coast of Asia Minor, was the site. The reason they gave was because there were hot and cold water springs at Bounarbashi, and Homer had mentioned two such springs in the twenty-second book of the *Iliad*.

So Schliemann went first to this remote village. His joy at setting foot on the Plain of Troy was severely modified when he discovered that the village was dirty and decayed. There was not the slightest air of nobility about the place, not the smallest hint of the grandeur that was Troy.

'This is not the site!' Schliemann said to himself, and proceeded to prove that it could not have been.

First he looked for the two springs, one as hot as fire, the other as cold as ice; and found, not two, but thirty-four! Furthermore, they all had a temperature of 17 degrees Centigrade . . .

Then he looked at the hill where Troy was supposed to have stood and at the rocky heights behind it. There *were* some small ruins at the southern end of the heights, but they were not on a Trojan scale. He remembered how, according to Homer, Achilles had chased Hector three times round the fortress, but when he tried to follow Hector's route he discovered at one point a drop so sheer that not even a mountain goat could have negotiated it.

Schliemann deduced from his copy of the *Iliad* that Troy could not have been more than three miles from the Hellespont (now called the Straits of the Dardanelles), whereas Bounarbashi was at least eight miles away. All the same, he hired workmen to sink several shafts over a wide area. They found only virgin soil and rock not far from the surface. That settled it.

Schliemann then began to search for other possible sites,

and at last came to a hill called Hissarlik, which was only three miles from the sea, at the north-west corner of a city which a Greek geographer called Strabo had called 'Novum Ilium' (New Troy).

Part of the hill was owned by the American Vice-Consul, Frank Calvert, who believed that Hissarlik was the site of Troy. Calvert had done some excavating and had found some rather impressive ruins, but he had been unable to persuade anyone to help him with more extensive work.

Schliemann began to assemble his evidence. The distance from Hissarlik to the Hellespont agreed with what Homer said. Hector and Achilles *could* have run three times round it. There were the ruins that Calvert had laid bare; and there was the fact that the later Greeks and Romans had believed that Troy lay hidden there. The absence of the two springs worried him for a time until it came to him that they might have dried up! He stood on the hill and looked toward the distant Mount Ida.

'From that summit,' he told himself, 'Jupiter gazed down on the city of Troy . . .'

During the next two years Schliemann spent some time in France and America. Before returning to Troy he decided, having divorced his first wife, that he would marry a Greek girl. He wrote to a friend in Athens and asked him to find a beautiful, well-educated, affectionate girl, who need not come from a wealthy family. The friend obliged, and Schliemann married Sophia Engastromenos in 1869, after giving her a short intelligence test!

He found some difficulty in obtaining a firman—permission to excavate—from the Turkish authorities, but he was not the man to let such a thing stand in his way for long. Soon all was in order and, after some preliminary excavations in 1870, he returned to Hissarlik the following year, accompanied by Sophia. She was as excited as her husband at the thought of what they might find.

Schliemann set up his headquarters in a village not far from Hissarlik, and engaged eighty workmen. On October

11 they began digging a trench on the steep northern slope of the hill. The upper levels held little interest for Schliemann. His one aim and object was Homer's Troy, and he had neither time nor inclination to make accurate records of the first finds. Later he came to realize how important it was to make scientific records, but in the early days he cut through or destroyed anything which prevented him from reaching his objective.

After a month's work they had to stop for the winter, and the Schliemanns returned to Athens until March the following year.

This time the labour force was nearly doubled. An engineer was engaged to make plans and maps. Schliemann built a wooden house on top of the hill, and he and Sophia lived on the spot.

As the digging continued, the trenches got deeper on the north side, and a huge platform was dug out many feet below the surface. Bedrock was reached some fifty feet down. When Schliemann surveyed the result of their work it was evident that the many levels represented different Troys, that one city had been built on top of another.

How could he identify *the* Troy? It must be in one of the deeper, earlier levels, he reasoned, for the Trojan War had been fought as long ago as 1,184 B.C. But the puzzling thing was, though Troy was a mighty city, the most impressive remains were all in the upper, later levels.

Schliemann decided that he might get more direct evidence on the south side of the hill, so the whole digging process was repeated there. Tons of earth were removed, a platform was constructed, ruins that were in the way were demolished, though notes and drawings were made of all the many pots, coins, statuettes and weapons that were turned up. In spite of trouble with the workmen, the hazards of the climate, and the danger from collapsing masonry, the work went on. Then Schliemann became ill with a fever, and work was abandoned for the rest of the season.

However, the dauntless archaeologist and his wife were

back early in 1873, making the best of the bad conditions under which they were forced to live. Schliemann did his best to suppress his disappointment at not having so far found the Troy of his dreams. After all, he tried to console himself, if nothing else came to light he had proved that Hissarlik was an archaeological site of great interest. The seven cities (actually, there were nine) reaching down through the strata were witness to that. But, he asked himself a thousand times, where was *his* Troy?

Then, in April of that year, while excavating to the west of some great walls which he had, in a spasm of wishful thinking, called the 'Great Tower of Troy', a beautifully paved, wide street appeared from beneath the rubble.

A street like that, Schliemann thought, *must* lead to a building of some importance. He immediately put the labourers on to removing the deep layer of wood-ash mixed with bricks and stones that covered the paving-stones, and soon they came across the remains of a large stone building. Nearby there were two gates standing twenty feet apart, and these too had been hidden by burned bricks and ash. Surely this was the Scaean Gate, and the building behind it the palace of King Priam! Was this, then, the end of his long search? Was this all that was left of Troy?

The gates were much smaller than he had imagined they would be, but perhaps Homer had been guilty of poetic licence when he had given the impression of great size and strength. Again there was that feeling of disappointment, though slighter this time. Schliemann decided to bring the excavations to an end in a few weeks' time.

But luck, which had befriended Schliemann so often in the past, came to his aid again, for on the day before he had planned to leave Troy for ever he stumbled on one of the greatest hoards of treasure ever found.

He was idly inspecting the burned masonry of one of the walls of 'Priam's Palace', nearly thirty feet below ground level, when he noticed what appeared to be a large copper object. He took a closer look, and his heart gave a great

lurch. That gleam behind the dust and grime was not copper
—it was, it could only be, gold!

He made sure that no one had been watching him, then
called Sophia to his side. He told her that the men had
to be got off the site, he didn't mind how it was done,
but go they must. Sophia did what he asked in the only
possible way. She paid the men off, and they did not argue.
They had no objection to doing nothing and receiving money
for it . . . Soon Schliemann and Sophia were alone among
the ruins.

Schliemann started to dig out the golden object with a
long knife. When the first one was free, another followed,
and then another. He was oblivious of the danger from the
huge blocks of stone, shored up by wooden beams, which
towered over him and which at any moment might collapse
and crush him to death. As each precious thing appeared
he handed it to his wife and she put them in her red shawl.

There were bracelets, goblets and bottles, buttons and
ornaments all of gold, gold bars, thousands of rings, ear-
rings, bronze weapons, and, most breathtaking of all, two
golden diadems hung with delicate chains which had adorned
the brow of the fortunate wearer. The larger of the diadems
contained over sixteen thousand pieces of gold in the form
of rings and leaf shapes.

'This is King Priam's treasure!' Schliemann declared, his
imagination plunging back to the scene during the last hours
of the burning city.

He could see it all. The treasure had been hastily gathered
together to save it from the flames. But the bearers had
obviously not reached a place of safety. They had abandoned
their precious burdens, and whatever had happened to them,
the gold had been left behind—only to be hidden under the
rubble when the walls and buildings collapsed.

Who had once worn the diadems, necklaces and ear-rings?
Well, why not Helen of Troy, whose beauty was legendary?
Schliemann thought it more than likely, and when later
Sophia was photographed wearing some of the gleaming

relics which enhanced her dark Greek beauty, he doubted whether even the fair Helen of old had looked more magnificent.

The story of Schliemann and Troy has a wry ending, for the brutal fact was that he had *not* found Troy, nor the Scaean Gate, the palace of Priam, nor even Priam's treasure. Or rather, he had found Troy, and had not recognized it, which makes the story even more pathetic.

The city which Schliemann had called Troy was the second-level city which had actually flourished in the third millenium B.C. The individual pieces of the treasure hoard were later proved to have originated in many different places and were probably part of the spoils of a war in which the city had been destroyed by fire.

Later archaeologists, including Schliemann's own assistant and, more recently, Professor Carl Blegen, have shown that the city of the sixth level was levelled by a violent earthquake, and that it was on the ruins of this city that Homer's Troy had been built, about 1,200 B.C.

Heinrich Schliemann died in 1890, after many more years of archaeological research and many more wonderful discoveries. His body lay in state in Athens, and even the King of Greece went to pay his respects to the odd little man who had combined obstinacy with vision and who had put to shame the stick-in-the-mud scholars who had laughed at him for believing in the reality of Troy.

Over his coffin in the hall of his palace at Athens a marble bust of Homer was placed; the poet whose words had provided Schliemann with the inspiration and determination to bring a buried city to life and to give flesh and blood to the ancient heroes who had walked the earth.

CHAPTER SEVEN

THE GOLDEN PHARAOH

BETWEEN the cliffs on the west bank of the Nile, opposite the modern city of Luxor in Egypt, lies the Valley of the Kings. The name suggests grandeur, but it is in fact a desolate place, with no trees or greenery to provide protection from the relentless sun which burns the rocks and the desert where once stood the magnificent city of Thebes.

The Valley of the Kings was the burial ground of the Egyptian kings and queens of the New Kingdom, during the eighteenth and nineteenth dynasties, from about 1,573 to 1,090 B.C. Before then royal tombs had been placed inside pyramids, huge monuments built over the burial chambers in which lay the bodies, surrounded by grave-goods of inestimable value. Though the pyramids were carefully guarded, and 'puzzle-passages' were made to confuse illegal entrants, robbers frequently plundered the tombs, risking the most terrible punishments for the sake of the hidden treasures.

The first king to choose a burial site in the Valley of the Kings was Tuthmosis I, at the beginning of the eighteenth dynasty. He instructed his architect to choose a remote spot in the Theban Hills and there hollow a tomb from the rock. It was his wish that his body should be taken to its last resting-place secretly, at dead of night, there to lie for ever, he hoped, undisturbed by robbers lusting after gold.

But the king was over-optimistic. In spite of all his precautions, his tomb *was* plundered, and so were those of the many kings who followed his example and chose 'secret' tombs in the valley. The robberies reached their peak in the twentieth dynasty.

In desperation the priests tried to save the bodies of their royal masters and mistresses by removing them from the single tombs and putting them together into a communal grave. The manoeuvre was successful. The royal mummies were undisturbed until 1881, when one was found by three brothers. After rifling the tomb they quarrelled over the share-out, and the disgruntled one got his revenge by revealing the whereabouts of the tomb to a German antiquarian named Emil Brugsch. Another tomb containing thirteen mummies was found by a French Egyptologist in 1898.

In 1902 an American, Theodore Davies, got permission to dig in the Valley of the Kings. He made some interesting discoveries, including the coffin and mummy of King Ahkenaten, and objects such as potsherds, seals and cups. Among the latter was a faience cup bearing the name Tutankhamun, and there was also a broken wooden box with the same name on it. But after digging in the valley for twelve years Davies decided that it had nothing more to offer, and he gave up his concession.

One of his assistants was the Chief Inspector of Antiquities for Upper Egypt. His name was Howard Carter, and he had for a long time wanted to excavate for himself in the Valley of the Kings. When Davies gave up, Carter's chance came. He teamed up with the wealthy Lord Carnarvon, who applied for, and was given, the concession to dig by the Egyptian Government.

People on all sides warned them that they would be wasting their time, but the two Englishmen carried on, undeterred. Carter was convinced that the tomb of the mysterious Tutankhamun lay somewhere in the valley, just as he was sure that the small tomb in which Davies had found the king's name was too insignificant to be that of a king of the eighteenth dynasty.

Tutankhamun was to keep his privacy for a few more years, though. No sooner had Carter and Lord Carnarvon completed their plans for the excavation than the First World War broke out, and they were only able to do some very spasmodic digging. It was not until the autumn of 1917 that Carter could begin to clear a way through great heaps of rubble. He made a map of the whole area, divided it into squares, and began to investigate each square separately and systematically.

For six years the work continued, but he found nothing of great importance. It seemed as though those who had said the valley had no more secrets to give up had been right. There was, however, one area that had not been fully excavated, and this lay near the tomb of King Rameses VI, already opened.

At the foot of the tomb was a pile of soil and boulders on which stood some huts built by the workmen who had made the tomb. Carter had to leave this last section untouched in order not to inconvenience the stream of tourists to the tomb, which was one of the most popular attractions in the valley. If he had been content to leave this small area for good the story would have fizzled out like a damp squib.

By 1922 Lord Carnarvon had had enough of the Valley of the Kings. Carter visited him at his home, Highclere Castle, and was told that work in the valley must stop. It was costing far too much, and the results had not nearly justified the money spent. This was a severe blow to Carter, who still believed fervently in the existence of the elusive tomb. He asked to be allowed one more season's digging. He reminded Lord Carnarvon of the one still unexplored site by the tomb of Rameses, and suggested that if he worked there out of the tourist season he would be in nobody's way.

Lord Carnarvon agreed to one more season, though with little enthusiasm. He was insistent that it must *be* the last . . .

So, on October 28, 1922, Carter arrived in Luxor, still full of hope, but little realizing how soon he was to achieve success beyond his dreams.

The discovery happened suddenly. On the first day the ancient huts were pulled down. The next task was to dig the ground beneath them. When Carter arrived at the site the following morning he immediately sensed an atmosphere of excitement among the workmen. He soon found out why. Underneath the site of the first hut they had found a step cut into the rock. Just one step, but tremendously significant. When more debris had been cleared it was seen that the step was just the first of a sunken stairway.

Carter caught the general excitement. Were they about to find a finished tomb or an incomplete one? If it were a tomb, would it have been robbed? If not, would there be a mummy, or would it have been taken to the safety of a communal tomb? Would it be *the* tomb? Carter's mind was awhirl with a jumble of thoughts and questions. The tension grew.

The steps in the rock finally turned into a roofed passage ten feet high. Then, at the level of the twelfth step, the top of a doorway appeared, plastered and sealed. Carter examined the seals eagerly, hoping to learn the name of the tomb's occupant. All he could see was the sign of the dog Anubis crouching over nine captive enemies of Egypt, which was the seal of a royal cemetery.

There was no doubt, then, that the tomb belonged to a very important person. It had obviously been undisturbed since the workmen's huts above it had been made during the twentieth dynasty.

It was infuriating to have to stop work for the night, but the hour was late and the labourers were exhausted. Carter did manage to bore a small hole through the wooden lintel of the door and he shone his torch through. He saw that the passage on the other side was filled with stone and rubble, a way of protecting what was beyond from marauders, and apparently a successful way.

Much as he longed to carry on without delay, Carter felt that it was only fair to let Lord Carnarvon know of the satisfactory progress they were making. He telegraphed his patron with the news that he had made a wonderful discovery and would await his arrival. He waited impatiently for two weeks, and Lord Carnarvon joined him on November 23.

When the full length of the door was revealed there were more seals further down it, and they bore the name of Tutankhamun . . .

Carter's first assumption that the tomb had not been robbed had to be revised, for the seals had in fact been broken, and afterwards repaired. This indicated that robbers had got into the tomb but had probably been caught before they could carry away all the contents. So far all was well. But Carter's elation received a jolt when the last of the rubbish blocking the stairs had been cleared away. Among it were some potsherds and boxes, the latter with the names of several kings, including that of Tutankhamun, on them.

Was this, then, going to turn out to be another communal tomb, shared by several royal persons? The only way to be sure was by opening the door of the tomb itself.

This meant clearing the rubble-filled passage, and it took several days before they had penetrated thirty yards along it and arrived at the second door, also sealed. It was a moment of almost unbearable anxiety. Years of disappointments and frustration could end in either fiasco or glory. Which was it going to be?

Carter made a small hole in the top of the door and poked an iron testing-rod through it. There was a space on the other side, not a high pile of rubble. He lit a candle. The flame flickered as air from the chamber beyond the door rushed out, but it did not go out. So the air did not contain poisonous gases.

The hole was enlarged, and Carter peered through. Behind him Lord Carnarvon and his daughter, and the assistants on the dig waited tensely. Only the sound of their breathing broke the eerie silence of centuries. Then Lord Carnarvon could bear it no longer.

'Can you see anything?' he asked impatiently.

This was Carter's greatest moment. Reluctantly he turned from his peephole. He tried to speak but had to steady his quivering voice before he could say simply, 'Yes, wonderful things.'

The wonderful things were revealed in all their rich profusion when the door was actually opened. The room itself, with bare, whitewashed walls, was about twenty-six feet long and twelve feet wide. Its contents were piled in haphazard heaps as though a whirlwind had hit a museum. There were three golden couches, their sides shaped like strange, long-legged beasts; caskets, both painted and inlaid, beds, chairs, a golden throne, shrines, dismantled chariots lying on their sides, boxes, trunks containing clothes and jewellery, bunches of flowers and boxes of food.

In their excitement Carter and Lord Carnarvon did not at first notice one important thing that was missing, but soon it dawned on them that there was no coffin in the chamber . . .

The old doubt assailed them—was it a tomb they had found, or simply a cache of hidden treasure? Then they saw that against one wall were two life-sized, black-varnished statues of kings, wearing kilts of gold, golden headdresses adorned with the sacred cobra, and each held a mace and a staff. The statues were face to face as though standing sentinel. And in the wall between them was yet another sealed door, the third!

The chamber they were in was only the antechamber. Behind the third door there surely must be the sarcophagus of Tutankhamun . . . Or perhaps there was a succession of rooms before the actual burial chamber.

The third door was not as solid as the first two, and Carter was eager to remove the plaster at once and get to the end of their search. But he realized that priority must be given to dealing with the contents of the ante-chamber. Before leaving the door, however, it was examined with the aid of powerful electric lamps, and a small opening near the bottom was noticed. It had been filled up and re-sealed, and it was evidence that robbers had penetrated beyond it, having first got into the antechamber.

Why had they bothered to go further than the ante-chamber when they had obviously failed to make off with the wealth of valuables lying all around them? What were they after that they so casually ignored the heaps of gold at their feet? There must have been something beyond the third door of such unbelievable magnificence that they had no eyes for anything else. Had they found it—or had they been caught redhanded by the guards? Carter hoped des-perately that the latter had happened.

Soon another discovery was made. While exploring the antechamber Carter knelt down and peered beneath one of the three golden couches. In the wall behind it was a hole, almost big enough for a man to crawl through. One of the lamps was dragged to him, and they shone it through the hole. The light revealed a small side-chamber or annexe, and it was full of boxes, baskets, vases and furniture, but everything was in total disorder.

The robbers, frantically searching for small articles of value, had broken some things, overturned others, and had even casually tossed some of them into the antechamber. The whirlwind had been at work in the annexe too . . .

Before the mystery behind the third sealed door could be solved there was an immense amount of work to be done. The tomb was blocked up while Carter made plans for the contents of the antechamber to be removed, cata-logued and preserved, and an army of experts moved in to help.

It was re-opened in the middle of December. Each object was handled and examined with the utmost care. Some of them were in a good state of preservation, but others were so fragile they threatened to crumble at a touch. The robes, sandals and funeral garlands, for instance, would disintegrate very quickly unless they were immediately treated with a preservative. Paraffin wax was used to cover many of the delicate things; others were sprayed with a cellulose solution.

It was not until February 1923 that the whole of the antechamber was cleared. Three months later thirty-four large packing-cases were loaded on to a steam-barge on the Nile for their seven-day journey to Cairo.

The 'spring-cleaning' had been a long, slow process, and it had not been made easier by the constant stream of officials and their friends to the tomb. Not only did they hold up the work, they also created a dangerous situation in which it was easy for an over-eager visitor to break the more fragile things that were piled up in the chamber.

Newspaper reporters from all over the world hurried to the Valley of the Kings, and the name of Tutankhamun became a household word. Carter's attitude to some of the more demanding visitors was less than welcoming, and he quickly earned a reputation for rudeness and surly bad manners. The atmosphere in the tomb was frequently explosive, and Carter and Lord Carnarvon came in for further criticism when, in an attempt to stem the flow of newspapermen, the right to report progress was given only to *The Times*.

But somehow progress *was* made and the antechamber cleared, and the time came to open the third door and discover what the two splendid statues had been guarding so zealously for thousands of years.

In the antechamber about twenty invited guests were sitting on chairs. Some were fellow archaeologists, others were officials of the Egyptian Government. And, of course, there was the representative of *The Times*, with pencil poised!

Early in the afternoon of February 17 Carter and Lord Carnarvon began to chip away the filling from the blocked door. The visitors watched in dead silence. No one dared to speculate on what might be on the other side.

When Carter had made an opening big enough to poke his torch through, something so completely unexpected met his eyes that he could only gasp in wonder. Through the small opening there seemed to be a wall of solid gold!

Whichever way the light twisted there was the dull gleam. As more stones were carefully removed, more of the wall was exposed. Then Carter climbed through the opening and found himself in a passage, little more than a foot wide, between the wall of the antechamber and the golden wall. By now the onlookers were buzzing with excitement. News that a major discovery was imminent had filtered through to the crowds outside the tomb.

Carter soon realized that the wall was part of a shrine built over the sarcophagus of the king, and so big that it practically filled the chamber in which it stood. He was actually standing in the burial chamber—at last.

Gold covered the shrine completely. Its sides were inlaid with panels of blue faience containing symbols for the protection of the dead. On the plastered walls of the chamber were ritual paintings. In the narrow passage between the shrine and the walls were funerary gifts and emblems such as wine jars, lamps, baskets, images of gods, and the seven magical oars which had been thought would assist the king on his journey to the next world.

Two doors stood at the eastern end of the shrine; bolted, it was noted, but not sealed. Did this mean that the robbers had in fact come as far as this, and had perhaps even opened the shrine itself? With great trepidation Carter drew the bolts and opened the doors.

To everyone's relief there was another gilded door leading to a shrine within the shrine, and the doors to this were bolted *and* sealed. So the king's body had not been disturbed. Beyond those sealed doors they were about to see the coffin containing the mummified body . . .

It was a moment that inspired both awe and a kind of fear. Even Carter, within reach of achieving his life's ambition, felt strangely reluctant to take the next step. To have opened the second shrine without careful planning might have resulted in damage to the first, so he decided to make a more detailed inspection of the burial chamber.

There was yet another door in the north-east corner. This led to a room which Carter called the 'Treasury', for it contained a host of splendid articles that were part of the funerary gifts. The most important of them was a huge chest entirely covered with gold-leaf and inscribed with hieroglyphic texts. Four goddesses guarded it, their arms outstretched protectively, their heads turned towards it.

Inside the chest was another one, of alabaster, containing four jars each with a stopper in the shape of the king's head. These were canopic jars which contained the mummified intestines of the king. According to Egyptian custom the embalmers would have removed them from the body before starting their work.

Anubis, the jackal-god, resting on a ceremonial sledge, was a sinister figure just inside the doorway of the burial chamber. Behind it was a bull's head, life-size. There were some model boats, fully rigged, lying around, articles of furniture and pieces of chariots.

With so many startling discoveries made in one day, it was very frustrating for Carter and Lord Carnarvon to realize that it would be unwise to start opening up the second shrine straightaway. But the hot Egyptian summer was beginning, and to expose the delicate objects to the heat was too risky. They had to contain their eagerness for another year. Never had the patience of an archaeologist been so tested.

The following months were marred by several unfortunate incidents. There were differences with the Egyptian Government about whom the finds belonged to; the coolness between Lord Carnarvon and the Press got distinctly colder, for they resented what they called his high-handed attitude; and there was even a serious disagreement between Carter and Lord Carnarvon, resulting in a vow never to work together again. Then, in the spring of 1923, Lord Carnarvon died from pneumonia caused by a mosquito bite that turned septic.

His death produced the stupid legend of the 'Mummy's Curse'; a piece of nonsense probably thought up by a journalist. The legend was fed by rumour and gossip, and for years afterwards whenever somebody who had even been remotely connected with the excavation died, the newspapers revelled in gruesome headlines and resurrected the story of the supposed curse.

Some members of Lord Carnarvon's family did indeed die suddenly and violently, but Tutankhamun cannot really be blamed. And why, one might ask, was Carter spared to live another sixteen years? Surely he should have been the first to be struck down!

The work of dismantling the golden shrines began in the autumn of 1924, and it proved to be very difficult. Not only was the shrine with the unbroken seals inside the biggest shrine, but inside that was another, and inside that another! Each one of the four was more magnificent than the one containing it. Between them were the magic objects the king needed on his journey, including lamps to light his way, jars of ointment, bows and arrows, and a fly-whisk made from ostrich feathers.

As each shrine was removed and the thrilling climax drew near, excitement mounted to an almost unbearable pitch. Carter removed the seals from the fourth shrine and opened the doors. There, almost filling the whole space, was the mighty sarcophagus, made of quartzite, and with a lid of yellow-tinted granite. On it was the name of Tutankhamun. Four goddesses, one at each corner, were carved in high relief.

When the granite lid, which weighed several hundredweights, was raised with block and tackle, the agony of expectation among the prominent people who had been invited to witness the last act of the drama brought stifled gasps. There had been many awe-inspiring moments during the long, drawn-out revelations of the glories of the tomb, but this one was the pinnacle, the culmination of all the hopes and fears of many years.

Inside the great stone coffin was something bulky, wrapped in linen. When the cloth was removed the coffin itself was revealed, with a golden effigy of the king on its lid. His hands, folded across his breast, held a crook and a flail, the emblems of royalty. The golden face had eyes made of aragonite and obsidian, two varieties of brightly coloured glass. The brow was lapis lazuli, and on it had been placed a tiny wreath of flowers, withered but still retaining slight traces of colour; a final tribute to the dead king, perhaps, from somebody who had loved him. It was a human touch in the midst of such grandeur that moved Carter deeply, and made him feel how close the past is to the present.

Even at this eleventh hour things could go wrong, and did. Carter, tired of the interference of the Egyptian Government in his conduct of the excavation, declared that he would close the tomb and abandon the whole project. A long and bitter quarrel led to a lawsuit when Carter sued the Egyptians and his lawyer accused them of behaving like bandits. It was not until November 1924, when the British Government took a hand in the affair, that Carter, who had in the meantime gone on a world lecture tour, was allowed to continue his work in the tomb. Early in 1925 the team of excavators was back in the valley.

When the lid of the coffin was lifted a second coffin was revealed, also linen-shrouded. This too was an effigy of the king, covered with garlands of petals, flowers and leaves, and even more splendidly golden than the first. It was also surprisingly heavy, and took eight men to lift it from its case. The reason for the heaviness was that there was a third coffin inside the second!

When the decaying shroud was taken off it was found to be, not a wooden affair coated with gold leaf, as the others had been, but made of solid gold studded with semi-precious stones . . .

Carter knew that inside this last magnificent box he would find the mummy. His feelings as the lid was lifted off by its golden handles could not be expressed in words, as he later said. He had seen beauty and priceless treasure at every

Gold mask of Tutankhamun

stage of the excavation. But now there would be something simple and human, the remains of the young king, and not a very important one, who had died about 1,350 B.C., at the age of eighteen. How strange that such an obscure person had been buried in this fabulously magnificent way!

When the gold coffin was finally opened the climax was tinged with sadness. The mummy, covered with linen wrappings, had a golden death mask covering the head and shoulders. But the mask was in marked contrast to the figure it covered, for the embalmers had been too lavish with their preserving oils, with the result that both the shroud and the body had become carbonised. They were hard and brittle, and the mummy had stuck to the bottom of the coffin so that it had to be chiselled away.

There were many treasures scattered about the body, and more than a hundred pieces of jewellery were found in the wrappings. It took nearly twenty pages of Carter's report to list them all!

When the jewellery had been removed and the last linen wrapping had been carefully loosened, Tutankhamun's face was exposed to the men who had been searching for him for so long. It was a gentle face, serene and cultured. The features were well-formed, and the lips clearly marked.

Everybody who saw it was impressed by the youthful beauty and the peaceful expression. The face also bore a remarkable testimony to the skill and artistry of the men who had created the effigies of the king, for they had represented him with extraordinary accuracy.

When Tutankhamun's body had been thoroughly examined it was returned to the burial chamber, there to stay for all time.

Today you can see the treasures, looking as splendid as they did in the time of Tutankhamun, in the Egyptian Museum in Cairo. Howard Carter died in 1939. His name will live as long as that of the king who died more than three thousand years before him. Tutankhamun was responsible for the greatest hoard of treasure ever found; and to Howard Carter we owe the most heart-stirring and romantic episode in the story of archaeology.

CHAPTER EIGHT

LABYRINTH!

ARTHUR EVANS was born in 1851, when Heinrich Schliemann was twenty-nine years old. After leaving Oxford he spent several years abroad, and became the Special Correspondent in the Balkans for the *Manchester Guardian*. His adventures read like a kind of spy story, thrilling but too fantastic.

On one occasion he swam naked, except for his hat, across a flooded river. (He wore the hat to keep his pencil and notebook in!)

In 1883 he and his wife toured Greece and paid a call on the Schliemanns. The German told him about his efforts to look for pre-Homeric sites at Knossos, which was a few miles south of the modern port of Heraklion on Crete, the largest island in the Mediterranean Sea.

In 1878 a Cretan merchant, while digging in his olive grove, had uncovered the foundations of a building and some large earthenware jars. An American newspaperman named Stillman heard of this, and helped the merchant to explore a number of narrow passages and cell-like rooms full of debris. The publicity that followed caused the Turkish authorities to forbid all further exploration of the site.

Schliemann, who had read Stillman's accounts in *The*

Times, had tried to buy the site, but he could not get permission to excavate.

In 1899, nine years after Schliemann's death, Evans succeeded in buying a quarter of the land he wanted. In the fields and vineyards he began the work that was to last the next twenty-five years, and to result in discoveries of a lost people and their lost world that pushed back the beginnings of European history another fifteen hundred years.

During the six years before the excavations started, Evans, who had been appointed Keeper of the Ashmolean Museum at Oxford, had become interested in seals which bore characters similar to hieroglyphs. His intention was to find out all he could about the kind of picture-writing he believed had been used in Europe in prehistoric times, and this led him more and more towards Crete. He had visited the island several times, and had collected a number of ancient seals and cameos which peasant women wore as charms, and some broken terracotta vases, and he had looked casually into some broken tombs.

When he began digging at Knossos in the spring of 1900 he meant to spend only a season or two on the island. As his excavations began to produce the remains of a civilization older than the Mycenaean, and one which had no records except in legend and some references in Greek literature, he carried on year after year. He was a wealthy man, and with his own money and the help of funds raised in England he was able to continue. The total cost of the excavations and the restoration of Cretan glories was over a quarter of a million pounds.

The Greeks had known and told many stories about Crete. Zeus, the King of the Gods, they said, had been born in a cave on the snow-capped Mount Ida, which rises into the intensely blue sky in the centre of the island; and his tomb was in Mount Jutka, near the northern coast. But the most famous legend is that of Minos, king, lawgiver, and son of Zeus.

His power had stretched far beyond Knossos, his capital, and the galleys of his navy had patrolled the sea round the island, suppressing piracy and preventing invasion. In order to avenge the murder of his son Androgeus, which had taken place in Athens on the mainland, he went to war against that city, and forced the Athenians to send him seven youths and seven maidens every year as tribute. These unfortunates were then eaten by the Minotaur, a monster, half man and half bull, who lived in a vast maze, called the Labyrinth, beneath the great palace which had been built for the king by Daedalus, his 'Minister of Works'. (This was the same Daedalus who 'invented' the first flying machine when he made wings for himself and his son Icarus and attempted to fly from the wrath of Minos.)

The Minotaur was eventually slain by Theseus, son of Aegeus, King of Athens, with the assistance of Ariadne, King Minos's daughter. Theseus arranged to be one of the seven youths chosen by the messengers from Knossos. When the intended victims arrived on the island Theseus and Ariadne gazed at each other and straightway fell in love.

She gave him a ball of thread, one end of which he fastened to a nail at the entrance door of the Labyrinth, and then unwound it as he made his way through the twisting passages and blind alleys of the maze. He reached the centre, slew the Minotaur with his bare fists—though some say by a sword given to him by Ariadne—followed the thread back to the beginning, and Ariadne promptly fell into his arms.

The story, unfortunately, does not have a happy ending. Theseus deserted Ariadne, and she was carried off by Dionysus, another son of Zeus. The grief-stricken and repentant Theseus forgot to spread white sails on his ship, as he promised his father he would if his quest had been successful. When Aegeus saw Theseus's ship coming in with black sails he thought his son must be dead and threw himself into the sea . . .

Let us return now to more recent times, and to fact.

In 1900 thirty baggy-trousered Cretan workmen, watched by Evans and his assistants, began to sink the first test-pits into the mound or *kephala* at Knossos, and success attended their efforts right from the start. Within two months two acres of buildings had been exposed; and after two years, with more than a hundred men at work, they had uncovered more than six acres.

The palace was built in two wings round a great courtyard. A large quantity of clay tablets, bearing the same mysterious hieroglyphs as on the seals, turned up. Evans began to realize that his main task now was to uncover the whole of the once flourishing Cretan civilization to which he gave the name 'Minoan', after King Minos.

As the years went by not only the palace of Knossos was laid bare, but also the surrounding town. The remains of at least two other palaces, almost as large as the upper one, were freed from their centuries-old grave.

The later white stone palace was a confusion of halls, rooms and corridors, with stairways connecting the various levels. There was a throne room, with the high-backed stone throne still in place, council chambers, offices, workshops and storerooms. The royal family's private living quarters included a bathroom containing a terracotta bath; and the whole palace was served by an extensive and well-made drainage system. There was even a lavatory that could be flushed.

Evans considered that the first and earliest palace was built about 2,200 B.C., towards the end of the Early Minoan Age, on the site of a Neolithic settlement. It was protected by thick walls and a tower near the sea-gate.

The second palace belonged to the Middle Minoan Age, from 2,000 to 1,550 B.C. It was rectangular in shape, with a courtyard in the centre, and two important entrances at the north and south. The royal treasury and the throne room were in the west wing. The rooms in the eastern section were the king's private rooms, pillared reception halls and the queen's suite, which was gay with painted dolphins and

75

dancing girls. Deep trenches under the east wing were divided into storerooms for oil, grain and other foodstuffs. The pottery stores provided evidence of the high artistic quality of Minoan work. There were eggshell-thin cups, vases, bowls and pitchers, beautifully shaped and delicately painted.

When the third and last palace was built on the ruins of the second it was on an even larger scale. It contained a grand staircase which led to a colonnaded hall. You can walk down its flights today and imagine yourself a Cretan king, though cement columns have replaced the original wooden props. The walls of the hall were painted with a procession of young men crowned with lilies, walking among flowers and grass. Extra towers and guardrooms were built for defence purposes, and the sea-gate was strengthened.

The storage chambers were deep pits under the floor of the west wing, and were guarded by signs of the double axe, the *labrys*, one of the symbols of the mother-goddess of Crete. The double axe is often seen in conjunction with a bull's head on wall paintings and pillars. Bulls also appeared engraved on seals and as decorations on vases.

The kings of Crete were also its priests, and the palace was the centre of the island's religious life. The chief deity was a mother-goddess, whose other symbol was a snake.

The magnificence of the Late Minoan Age lasted until about 1,400 B.C., according to Evans, and the Cretan civilization reached its peak of prosperity and importance. Then, with the roar of an angry bull, an earthquake brought the palace and the other buildings tumbling to the ground, there to be destroyed by fire.

While layers of earth and rubble were being removed from the third palace some sensational discoveries were made. One of them was a mural, almost intact, which turned out to be the picture of a young man, a cupbearer, the first Minoan ever to be seen by twentieth-century eyes. He had broad shoulders and a slim waist; curly black hair, full lips and a noble profile. He wore a patterned girdle; the upper

76

part of his body was bare. The colours were as bright as though they had been painted the previous day. The figure was part of the procession of men and women walking in single file towards the palace, perhaps to take part in a religious ceremony, though only the cupbearer is complete.

The king's audience chamber was the next exciting find. The throne, made of gypsum, stood against the wall. There were stone benches on either side. On the floor was a litter of ornaments made of gold, crystal and lapis lazuli, an overturned oil jar and some broken vessels. This suggested that something or someone had rudely interrupted a sacred ceremony. Invaders? An earthquake? A disastrous fire?

The walls of the throne room were richly painted with river scenes; and green, red and blue griffins guarded the throne. An opening in the wall led to an inner chamber, the shrine of the mother-goddess.

As the excavations continued, other brilliantly coloured frescoes were found, depicting the life of the Minoan people, and the flowers, birds and animals they were familiar with. A monkey plucked saffron flowers, and a grey bird soared with outstretched wings over a rocky landscape.

We learn from the frescoes that Minoan women enjoyed a much freer life than most women of early times. There were few restrictions on them, and they had many opportunities for enjoyment. Their dresses were elaborate, and their jewellery brilliant. There was something very modern about their freedom and liveliness, their flounced skirts and puffed sleeves, and the little curls across their foreheads.

A particularly interesting, though puzzling, frieze showed a young man somersaulting over the back of a galloping bull. A girl stood in front of the animal and another behind it, waiting, it seemed, to steady the daring acrobat as he reached the ground. Bull-leaping must have been a very difficult and dangerous feat, if it was possible at all. But bull sports were an essential feature of Minoan life and were bound up with the worship of the mother-goddess. Perhaps the young athletes were war captives from Athens who were forced to risk, and often lose, their lives in attempting the impossible; not killed by a monster, as the legend says, but butchered (and gored to death) to make a Cretan holiday.

It is possible that the priest-king wore a mask over his face during certain religious observances (Cretan sealstones have such pictures engraved on them), thus giving rise to the legend of the Athenian men and maidens being eaten by the Minotaur. If this supposition is correct, then Theseus, in killing the Minotaur, had really killed King Minos!

The Labyrinth (the house of the labrys) can certainly be explained by the twisting corridors that turned the palace into a maze, and the shafts and tunnels of the drainage system that were big enough for a man to crawl through. Thus, it seems, was a legend born . . .

When a great deal of the palace had been excavated, Evans decided to try to reconstruct it as it had been in its glorious heyday. With the help of other archaeologists and architects the walls and columns were rebuilt, frescoes repainted, and the halls, staircases, galleries and ceremonial bathing-places arose from a tumbled heap of ruins to something approaching their former magnificence. Then, after many years' work, the palace was handed over to the Greek Government.

The work of restoration came in for much criticism from some archaeologists, who complained that Evans had used too much imagination, more than the actual finds justified, they said. He had used modern materials, such as reinforced concrete, that were unknown in the Minoan Age. There was so much new construction that it was difficult to see the original stones.

'The falsification of monuments by deceptive restoration verges on forgery,' Ernst Buschor, a German archaeologist, declared indignantly.

Of course Sir Arthur Evans was not a deliberate forger. If he went too far in his restoration of Knossos it was

Fresco from Knossos, showing bull-leaping

entirely due to his fanatical belief in his theories, and his life-long obsession with the civilization he had found and brought to life in all its vivid detail.

There is, at the moment, a splendidly acrimonious argument going on between archaeologists and philologists about the accuracy of Evans's dating of the various stages of the Minoan civilization.

For over fifty years scholars accepted Evans's findings, and they based their accounts of the early history of Europe on his framework. Though there had been rumblings of disagreement (chiefly from Professor Sir Alan Wace, a former Director of the British School at Athens, and Professor Carl Blegen, an American archaeologist from the University of Cincinnati), open 'warfare' did not break out until 1960. Then Professor Leonard R. Palmer, Professor of Comparative Philology at Oxford, led a brave, lonely attack on the widely held theory that Knossos had finally perished about 1,400 B.C.

Professor Palmer asserted that some of Evans's facts were wrong—that the actual records of the long excavation contradicted them; and he started a controversy that is likely to rage for a long time. He suggests that, while there was no question of deception, Evans's autocratic, and obstinate nature would not let him admit that he had only a hazy idea of what was going on at one stage of the work; and that he had, in consequence, made grave errors in interpreting the meaning of his finds.

Professor Palmer has examined Evans's own notebooks and the records made by his assistant, Duncan Mackenzie, and has pointed out what he thinks are serious discrepancies between them and the official accounts published later.

These mistakes, he says, make nonsense of the view that Knossos was destroyed in 1,400 B.C.; that the people overthrew their priest-king and in doing so brought their greatness to an end. Evans claimed that after this disaster the ruined palace was occupied by 'squatters', and that Crete was a poor, forgotten island until the Greeks arrived two hundred years later.

Professor Palmer's theory is that the Minoan kings ruled at Knossos until 1,400 B.C. and were then defeated by main-

Storerooms in the Palace of Minos of Knossos

land Greeks; that the Minoan civilization was replaced by the Mycenaean; and that, far from suffering from poverty and isolation, the Cretans enjoyed a great prosperity. Much of the palace was rebuilt, and trading with other countries was resumed. Knossos did not finally fall until 1,150 B.C., and then to the Dorians from Greece.

If Professor Palmer is right, then the early history of Greece and Crete will have to be re-written, and this will have important repercussions on the history of Europe and

81

the Near East. He is strongly supported by Professor Blegen. Evans is just as firmly upheld by Mr John Boardman, Reader in Classical Archaeology at Oxford. And the argument continues . . .

You will remember that Evans's first interest in Knossos was in finding seals with 'writing' on them. Those he had already gathered had signs such as arrows, stars, heads and hands, which might represent some kind of script. During the long excavation of the palaces he came across hundreds of inscribed clay tablets, but though he puzzled over them for forty years he never succeeded in deciphering the strange language.

There were two forms of writing on the tablets. Evans called them Linear A and Linear B, and more examples of the latter were found on the mainland of Greece. In 1939 Professor Blegen discovered 600 tablets at Pylos, a Mycenaean settlement, and since then more have turned up at Mycenae and other places.

The riddle of the Linear B script was solved ten years after Evans's death by a young architect named Michael Ventris. In 1936, when he was fourteen, Ventris had attended a lecture given by Evans, and had been fascinated by the old archaeologist's account of his discovery of the forgotten Minoan civilization on Crete and of the mysterious writing on the tablets. The boy was already interested in ancient languages, and there and then he made up his mind that he would break down the Cretan code.

Sixteen years later, by using the methods that broke down military codes, the brilliant amateur had succeeded where the experts had failed. Linear B was an early form of Greek, he discovered, five hundred years older than the language as Homer had written it. This seemed to prove that the Mycenaeans were themselves Greeks who had learned their language from the Minoans.

Nearly all the tablets were lists—of slaves, workmen, craftsmen, palace stores. Even the number of broken wine jars had been noted! Although there were no letters, poems or legends—such may yet be found, of course—it is now possible to reconstruct much more fully the life and times of the people who built up the glorious civilization of Crete.

The other script, Linear A, has not yet been deciphered. It is obviously a close relative of Linear B, perhaps an ancestor, but though a number of scholars are working on it not enough tablets are available for anything conclusive to be decided. Dr C. Gordon, an American scholar, claims that Linear A has a connection with the Accadian script used in Babylonia. Other experts suggest either a Semitic origin or one related to the early languages of Anatolia.

It is sad that Michael Ventris is not able to develop his work on the Linear B script or to tackle Linear A with the same mixture of imaginative understanding and brilliant reasoning. In 1956, in the same year that his book describing his discovery was published, he was killed in a car accident. He was only thirty-four.

CHAPTER NINE

LIONS AND LIBRARIES

IN 612 B.C. Nineveh, the capital city of the ruthless, war-loving Assyrians, who were the masters of a great empire between the rivers Tigris and Euphrates in Mesopotamia, fell to the invading Chaldeans and Medes and was destroyed.

In time the memory of Nineveh's power and magnificence grew dim. The prophets of the Old Testament looked back with satisfaction on its destruction and congratulated God for having brought to the Assyrians the punishment they deserved. But, like Ur, Babylon, and other ancient cities of the land between the two rivers, Nineveh became nothing but part of a legend. The ruins disappeared below the blown sand, and all that was left of it were huge mounds of dust and earth . . .

At the beginning of the nineteenth century Claudius James Rich, a Civil Servant stationed in Baghdad, was struck with the idea that a city might lie under a group of mounds which lay east of the Tigris and opposite the modern city of Mosul. He started a rather haphazard excavation which had disappointing results. His finds were small—a few clay tablets and pieces of pottery which he sent to the British Museum—and his death from cholera in 1820 put an end to his work.

Paul-Emile Botta, the French vice-consul at Mosul, was the next person to get bitten by the Nineveh bug. In 1842 he made some trial trenches at Küyünjik, with little success. The following year his excavation of a mound at Khorsabad, north of where Rich had dug, revealed the walls of a vast palace, the stone slabs of which were carved with figures of animals and men, scenes of battles and religious ceremonies, and with wedge-shaped writing that resembled the prints of birds. More than a hundred rooms, halls and corridors were gradually revealed. Botta was convinced that he had uncovered Nineveh.

As it turned out he was mistaken. What he had really found was the palace of another Assyrian city, one that had been built about 700 B.C. by Sargon II, the king who had raised Assyria to the height of its power as a military empire.

Botta continued his work under difficulties. The Turkish governor of the district was unfriendly and tried to prevent the excavation by pretending that Botta was smuggling treasures out of the country. His pretext had some truth in it, because Botta managed to get a load of sculptured slabs down the Tigris to the coast and then by sea to France. They can now be seen in the Louvre in Paris.

In 1848 Botta had to give up his researches when his government transferred him to North Africa. It was left to an Englishman named Austen Henry Layard to achieve the success that had eluded Rich and Botta.

Layard is one of the giants of archaeology of the nineteenth century. His parents wanted him to be a lawyer, but his adventurous, restless nature rebelled against law books. After six years in a solicitor's office he decided that life on his uncle's coffee plantation in Ceylon would be more to his liking. First, though, fascinated by the idea of the 'mysterious East', he would see as much of the world as he could before reaching Ceylon.

He travelled overland through Europe, partly on horseback, and through the Middle East, where adventures with brigands left him almost penniless. He found himself at last in Damascus, looking like a starving tramp.

Layard never did reach that coffee plantation because he fell in love with the awe-inspiring desolation of Mesopotamia. He met Botta, whose enthusiasm he caught, and was soon excavating for himself, after persuading the British Consul at Constantinople to provide the money for the work—the princely sum of £60!

The mound Layard chose was twenty miles south of Mosul. It was called Nimrud by the Arabs because they thought that the city underneath it had been built by Nimrod, the mighty hunter of the Genesis story, and the great-grandson of Noah. The local sheik provided Layard with a few men, and they set to work, digging into the biggest mound of the group.

At the end of the first day they had uncovered walls of rooms lined with alabaster slabs which were covered with the same wedge-shaped writing that Botta had come across. As time went on and the labour force was increased, more sculptured stones came to light. On them people with hooked noses, heavy eyelids and thick curly beards were fighting, burning, climbing the walls of cities, torturing prisoners, carrying away captives and treasure. These were Assyrians in action . . .

These discoveries were tremendously exciting, because nothing like them had ever been seen before. The excitement mounted feverishly when an enormous human head, carved out of alabaster, appeared, proud and fierce-looking.

'It is Nimrod himself!' cried the Arab workmen, and downed tools immediately. They celebrated the discovery with a feast that lasted well into the early hours of the next morning. Sheep were killed and eaten, and some wandering musicians provided dance music.

But the statue was *not* that of the legendary hero. When it was fully uncovered the human head had a lion's body, and wings. Then more winged lions, and huge bulls with human heads, to say nothing of winged humans and eagle-headed creatures, were hauled with difficulty out of their sandy grave.

Pairs of these figures, each weighing over ten tons, had formed the entrances to the halls and rooms of the palace, which it was later found had been built by an Assyrian king called Ashur-nasir-pal II, who had reigned between 884 and 859 B.C.

Some of the figures eventually reached London after a fantastic journey, first to the Tigris on home-made carts drawn by men because the buffaloes had jibbed at the task, then floated on rafts to Basra on the Persian Gulf, then by way of India and around the Cape of Good Hope. Now you can see them in their sinister grandeur in the British Museum.

Layard thought he had discovered Nineveh—indeed, he wrote a book called *Nineveh and its Remains*—just as Botta thought he had; but both men were mistaken. Nineveh really lay under the mounds where Rich had said it did, and where Botta had made his half-hearted attempt to dig!

Layard's city was the Calah of the Bible, the second of the three Assyrian capitals, and was built before Nineveh. During the excavations hundreds of tons of earth were removed by chanting Arabs, and three palaces were uncovered; that of Ashur-nasir-pal II, another built by his son Shalmaneser III (c. 859–824 B.C.), and the third by Esarhaddon (c. 680–669 B.C.).

In 1849 Layard turned his attention to the mound of Küyünjik, where Botta had failed to find anything of interest. Botta must have wished that he had not given up so easily, for he would have found what Layard found—Nineveh at last, and the palace of Sennacherib (c. 705–681 B.C.), the Assyrian king who is mentioned in the nineteenth chapter of the Second Book of Kings.

On the inner walls of the palace was a sculptured relief showing the siege of Lachish, a town named in the Old Testament story. It contained the usual violent incidents—war, plundering, torture, and the triumph of the invading

87

Winged man-headed bull from the palace of Ashur-nasir-pal II

Assyrians. The almost legendary Sennacherib was now an actual historical figure whose merciless cruelty was pictured on cylinders of clay and described in his own words.

The most important find at Nineveh, in the spring of 1850, was the Royal Library, in two rooms which had been added on to the palace. It consisted of thousands of clay tablets and six- to ten-sided cylinders, most of them broken or half burned, inscribed with the wedge-shaped writing we call cuneiform; and they covered the floor to a depth of more than a foot.

A few years later Layard's assistant, Hormuzd Rassam, found the ruins of another library in another palace built by Sennacherib's grandson, Ashur-bani-pal.

For years scholars at the British Museum worked on the tablets, which numbered more than twenty-five thousand altogether, fitting together the fragments and translating them. There were business contracts, letters, medical works, 'books' about the stars, science, botany, mathematics, religion, history, folklore, poems and legends. Most of them were copies of Babylonian books which Ashur-bani-pal, a studious and peace-loving man, had ordered to be made. One of them, the 'Gilgamesh Epic', was probably the first important written poem in the history of the world. It told the story of the hero, Gilgamesh, who was two-thirds god and one-third man, and his search for eternal life, and it contains an account of the Flood.

As the Gilgamesh Epic was written before the Bible story and is strikingly similar to it in many ways, it is clear that the latter came from Babylonian sources.

A key to cuneiform writing had already been found when the library was discovered—you can read how that was accomplished in the next chapter—and the vast amount of literature now at scholars' disposal led to a new and full knowledge of the Assyrians and the Babylonians. It also paved the way to the discovery of a hitherto unknown people, the Sumerians, whose story was eventually made clear by Sir Leonard Woolley.

There are two important aspects of Layard's work which need emphasizing. One is the crudity of methods of excavation in his day. Many objects which have lain for centuries in the ground tend to disintegrate when they are exposed to the air, and a hundred years ago the knowledge of how to preserve fragile or partly decayed things was not nearly as advanced as it is today. Layard found helmets, armour, and things made of glass and ivory, but because they fell to pieces or were so decomposed that he could not keep them intact they were thrown away. His references to the lost treasure in his reports show his casual attitude.

Nor was he careful with the contents of the two libraries. They were not packed properly, and many of them crumbled to pieces during their journey to England. Compare the extraordinary care that was taken with the articles found in the Sutton Hoo treasure ship in 1939, and you will appreciate the advance in techniques and the change in thinking that makes the present-day archaeologist regard a stain in sand as important as a ten-ton effigy.

The second thing to be noticed is the attitude of the British Government to archaeology—a parsimonious attitude that hasn't changed much in a hundred years!

The British ambassador to Turkey, Sir Stratford Canning, had the utmost difficulty in persuading the British Museum to advance £2,000 when it became obvious that Nimrud was a place that was going to yield great discoveries. Botta had received a much more generous allowance from the French Government. Layard's finds were sent to London in the most primitive way imaginable, and many objects were lost or broken *en route*. The French Government provided Botta with a naval vessel for the transportation of *his* treasures. Botta was helped by his government in the publication of his five-volume report. Layard was refused help by *his* government, and it was left to a private publisher to offer to put the plans and drawings before the public. In 1849 the British Museum *did* promise Layard £4,000 if he would continue his work at Nineveh, but cut £1,000 off the grant when he agreed!

The Ministry of Works 1968 budget for archaeological excavations and the laboratory work which is necessary afterwards was about £145,000. The purchase and upkeep of historic monuments cost even more; but archaeologists could do with ten times as much without feeling they were being greedy . . .

CHAPTER TEN

KEY TO CUNEIFORM

KNOWLEDGE of the ancient inhabitants of Mesopotamia was very fragmentary indeed before it was possible to decipher the writings they had left behind. It was all very well to stare at the huge palaces and platforms that excavators unearthed, and guess at the stories behind the sculptured scenes on walls and monuments, but not to *know* was very galling.

There were legends, of course. Herodotus, the Greek historian, and the authors of the Old Testament had provided a sketchy and not always accurate outline. But it was not until the ability to understand cuneiform writing was gained that these long-dead people came to life again. Then the details of their daily lives, their hopes and fears, their achievements in war and peace, their religion, customs and laws all sprang out of the cracked clay that had held them secret.

Shadows were given substance, and legends became history. Dark deeds were uncovered. Homes, schools, temples and palaces stood out squarely and sharply in a new sunlight; and slaves, craftsmen, merchants, nobles, priests and kings moved about their business before the newly opened eyes of the nineteenth and twentieth centuries.

The curious wedge-shaped characters of cuneiform writing

had intrigued and baffled scholars right up to the middle of the nineteenth century. A great number of clay tablets had accumulated, and no one could read them with any degree of accuracy, though there had been many early attempts to decipher the unknown language.

One of the pioneers was Karsten Niebuhr, a Danish traveller in the Near East in the eighteenth century. He sorted out the individual signs of the script and made a list of forty-two separate characters which he had copied from the ruins of the ancient Persian city of Persepolis. His conclusion was that the script was based on *letters*, not words, and that there were at Persepolis three different systems of writing.

Cuneiform writing

Niebuhr's findings, published in the 1770's, excited language students everywhere; and one of them, a German named Tychsen, was able in 1798 to add a further vital link to the chain. He identified one of the signs, an oblique wedge which constantly occurred, as a *word-divider*.

Another important advance was made by Georg Grotefend, an obscure young German teacher, who worked on the theory that some inscriptions contained the same text in three different languages, one of which might be Old Persian. It was his opinion that each group of signs stood for a *sound*, not a word. He succeeded in making out twelve different letters and the names of three Persian kings—Darius, Hystaspes and Xerxes. In 1802 he announced the results of his research in reports that were read before the Academy of Sciences in Göttingen, and they were afterwards published, but only in the local newspaper and then as an appendix to someone else's book.

93

In 1843, the year that Botta began his excavations at Khorsabad, an Englishman, who knew nothing of what Grotefend had discovered forty years before, succeeded in deciphering cuneiform writing on his own. This was Lieutenant (later Sir) Henry Rawlinson. He was a mixture of soldier and scholar who had studied Oriental languages and whose curiosity had been aroused by cuneiform.

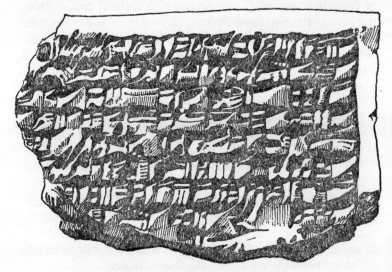

Fragment of inscribed clay tablet

There existed a huge piece of cuneiform script, carved on the face of a cliff at Behistun in Persia, on the caravan route from Babylon to Ecbatana. The carvings in relief showed King Darius with one foot on a defeated enemy, and before him a line of captives. Darius had ordered the enormous inscription to be made in 516 B.C. to show his power and the extent of his empire to all who passed by.

The picture was surrounded by columns of script—over a thousand lines altogether—and the whole thing, which measured 150 by 100 feet, was 300 feet from the ground.

The rock rose straight up from the plain like the jagged tooth of a giant, so that the inscriptions, written in three languages, were both difficult to see and to get at.

While Rawlinson was stationed in Persia, between 1835 and 1838, he climbed up the slippery surface of the rock as far as he could several times. He used ropes where the track was specially steep, and a plank to put across the deep ravines, and he copied as much of the inscription as he could see.

The first column, in Old Persian, was comparatively easy to reach, though ladders were needed to get to the upper part. Rawlinson had to haul a ladder on to an eighteen-inch-wide ledge, then stand on the topmost rung, steady his body against the rock with his left arm, hold his note-book in his left hand and his pencil in the other. It was a most uncomfortable position, and one slip would have meant hurtling to death down the precipice, but he managed to climb up and cling to his perch so often that soon all sense of danger left him.

Rawlinson had to leave Persia on military business, and it was not until 1844 that he could resume his quest. It was more difficult still to reach the recess which contained the second language, Elamite. On one side there was no ledge at all, and the other side could only be reached by using a ladder as a bridge across a deep chasm. However, after some ghastly moments, Rawlinson crossed the open space and took impressions of the writings by pressing wads of moistened paper against the rock-face. Later the casts were dried and packed up ready for the time when the work of translation could begin.

The Babylonian inscriptions caused even more trouble. The writing could be seen with the aid of a powerful telescope from below, but Rawlinson wanted to get a cast. He was not put off when goatherds who were used to tracking their animals over the face of the mountain declared that this particular spot was impossible to approach. Rawlinson was delighted when a Kurdish boy volunteered to make the attempt, and promised him a considerable reward if he succeeded.

The boy had to squeeze himself up a narrow cleft by the side of a projecting mass of rock. Then he drove a wooden peg into the cleft, tied a rope to it and tried to swing himself over to another cleft. But this manoeuvre failed, and he had to make the crossing by hanging on with toes and fingers and pass over a distance of twenty feet of almost smooth, perpendicular rock.

To the anxious watchers below it seemed that a miracle had happened when the boy reached the second cleft. He then drove in another peg, and, with a rope attached to the first one, managed to swing himself over the projection. With a short ladder fixed to the rope-swing he made himself a seat and, under Rawlinson's direction, took a paper cast of the Babylonian translation of the records of Darius.

This happened in 1847. Rawlinson had been able to read the Old Persian section of the inscription four years earlier, but the translation of the Babylonian section took many years, for Babylonian cuneiform was much more complicated.

Other scholars joined Rawlinson in studying the script, but for a long time there was confusion and a sense of defeat. In 1850 Rawlinson wrote that he was tempted to abandon the work altogether, but fortunately he changed his mind. The following year he put forward a theory that one sign in cuneiform script might be read in several different ways, its meaning depending on how it was placed in a word or a sentence. Other scholars disagreed. It was left to the Royal Asiatic Society of London to settle the matter in 1857.

W. H. Fox Talbot, who had already translated a piece of Assyrian writing from a clay cylinder of Tiglath-Pileser I, sent it to the Society with the suggestion that they should give the original text to Rawlinson and also to two other experts; that they should all submit their own translations in sealed envelopes to a committee; and that all the envelopes should be opened at the same time and the results compared.

Rawlinson and two scholars named Hincks and Offert agreed, and six weeks later the four entries were examined. The members of the committee drew up a report—and it was sensational! There were astonishing similarities between the four versions, and even where there were differences each translator had admitted that he was not sure about those particular passages. The key to cuneiform had at last, and without question, been discovered. There was then no barrier guarding the secrets of Mesopotamian civilization.

We cannot end the story of the decipherment of cuneiform writing without mentioning the later work of a remarkable man named George Smith. He was an engraver of banknotes who became a 'repairer' in the Oriental Department of the British Museum. He had a passion for the Museum's Assyrian objects which had arrived from Nineveh. When he read the books and articles written by Layard and Rawlinson he formed an unshakeable resolve to put together the broken pieces of the library tablets and translate them. The fragments were of all sizes, from half an inch to a foot long, and they were thickly coated with dirt. So the task was stupendously difficult.

George Smith had not received a good education. He was not an attractive person either in appearance or manner, and no one imagined for a moment that he would have either the skill to join the pieces together or the genius to decipher them. As it turned out, he became one of the leading experts on Assyria.

He started to work on the vast library in 1863, and eight years later he published a history of the reign of Ashur-banipal which he had found in some of the 'books'. In 1872 he discovered the Assyrian version of the story of Noah and the Flood in the Gilgamesh Epic, and its resemblance to the Bible story startled his audience when Smith described his discovery to the Society of Biblical Archaeology.

For years scholars argued about it. Some refused to believe that the Genesis writer had borrowed his material from an older legend which had a basis in something that had really happened. Others were annoyed that the Flood story was not just a myth invented by the Genesis writer for his own purpose. Meanwhile, George Smith became famous.

The Flood epic took up twelve clay tablets, but part of the eleventh, which Smith thought would contain about fifteen lines, was missing. The *Daily Telegraph*, hoping for a scoop, offered Smith a thousand guineas if he would lead an expedition to Nineveh and try to find the missing piece.

Smith's first thought was—talk about a needle in a haystack! But he agreed to try. He got leave of absence for six months from the British Museum and set off for Mesopotamia. The fantastic climax to the story is that, within a week, he found the missing fragment under an enormous pile of debris left by previous excavators at the bottom of a pit! The fact that it contained seventeen lines of script, instead of the estimated fifteen, did not lessen Smith's joy. And the *Daily Telegraph* got its scoop.

In 1874 the British Museum financed another expedition which Smith led, and several hundred more cuneiform tablets were recovered from the ruins of Nineveh. Another attempt two years later unfortunately ended in failure. Smith reached Mosul too late in the season to start digging. During the great heat of the summer he tried to cross the desert from Nineveh to the Mediterranean, but collapsed with dysentery and died in a shepherd's hut at Aleppo.

CHAPTER ELEVEN

WAR AT MAIDEN CASTLE

THOMAS HARDY, the chronicler of Wessex, could sit at his study window in his house in Dorchester and see, beyond the city's Roman walls, a long low hill. Its crest was broken by a series of huge mounds and ditches which coiled round it like that legendary dragon, the Lambton Worm. It dominated the surrounding countryside and impressed Hardy so strongly that he described it several times in vivid words like these: 'It may indeed be likened to an enormous many-limbed organism of an antediluvian time . . . lying helpless, and covered with a thin green cloth, which hides its substance while revealing its contour . . .'

This great hill-fort is Maiden Castle, the most famous earthwork in Britain. There is actually no castle connected with it. Its ancient name was Mai-Dun, or 'great hill'.

Religion and ceremony had nothing to do with Maiden Castle; it was concerned solely with war. The story of its excavation by Sir Mortimer Wheeler and his team of a hundred assistants between the years 1934 and 1938 is a story of the patience and eagle-eyed observation that must be part of a modern archaeologist's stock-in-trade.

They did not expect to find treasure, so they were not disappointed. No golden breastplate came to light, no glittering jewellery, nothing sensational or fabulous. But four years of carefully planned work methodically carried out, meticulous recording, and skilled sifting of evidence provided a new chapter in British history.

Maiden Castle today

The excavation of Maiden Castle is a classic example of how most scientific archaeological researches are carried out —with little drama or excitement, no chance discoveries by children or amateurs (or dogs!), no intuition or leaps in the dark; but by intelligence, hard work and perseverance.

The Society of Antiquaries of London provided more than £5,000 for the work, and the report afterwards published by the Society in 1943 emphasized its satisfaction with the results and its admiration for the workers. Before 1934 practically nothing was known about Maiden Castle. Now the chalk embankments and filled-in ditches have revealed a tangled story that began in the Late Stone Age and only came to an end some 2,000 years later, at the beginning of the Christian era.

The hill known as Maiden Castle is crowned by two small mounds. On the eastern one the Neolithic people who lived and farmed in southern England dug two flat-bottomed ditches about five feet deep which covered ten acres or so, and with causeways crossing them. Such a causewayed camp, of which there are about a dozen known in southern England, was an enclosure used more to keep cattle from straying than as a protection against enemies.

The farmers also dug cooking-pits in the chalk. Sir Mortimer Wheeler found flint and bone tools and pieces of round-bottomed pots in the pits and ditches.

The settlement was abandoned after some time, but soon afterwards the site was used again, about 1,500 B.C., also by Neolithic people, as a great burial mound, the longest barrow known in England. It was originally about six feet high, sixty feet broad, and a third of a mile in length. On either side there was a ditch, twelve feet wide. Towards the eastern end of the barrow a grave was excavated, and the body of a man was found—or rather, parts of a body, because the man's legs, arms and head had been hacked off, and his skull had been opened. Presumably the brain had been cut out and eaten.

This mysterious and brutal assault on a dead man seems to indicate that he had been the victim of a ritual feast. In other words, our ancestors had practised cannibalism as part of their religion.

From time to time other people, such as the Peterborough Folk and the Beaker Folk, occupied the hill, as we know from the potsherds found in the ditches of the long barrow. The people of the Bronze Age—the Food Vessel People and the Urn People—preferred the valleys to the hill-top. For about twelve hundred years Maiden Castle was again abandoned. Trees grew on it, and only the occasional hunter climbed the slopes and disturbed the silence.

During the Early Iron Age, about 300 B.C., immigrants who had been driven from their homes in north-east France by famine or enemies landed on the Wessex coast. Some of them chose Maiden Castle, with its commanding position and long views, as a base for their defence works.

As a start they fortified the Neolithic cattle corral. They built a wall of earth and chalk, from ten to twelve feet high, and just as wide, round the area, now extended to sixteen acres, and reinforced it with timber posts five feet apart. Outside the wall was a ditch fifty feet wide and twenty feet deep.

Behind the wall a village grew up. The inhabitants lived in rectangular wooden huts, stored their food in pits, and lived quietly and peacefully enough, for there is no evidence of any attack. The thick walls fell down eventually through old age!

When, about 200 B.C., the population had grown so that the village was no longer big enough, it was extended westwards until forty-six acres were covered altogether, and another wall and ditch were added. But the new wall was constructed to a different pattern.

The rampart did not have a vertical face, but sloped deeply down to the ditch. This would present greater difficulties for invaders, for they would find it more exhausting to scale the glacier-like slope than to arrive unhindered at a wall, and they would be more at the mercy of the spears and arrows of the defenders. The double gates at the east end were also strengthened by a barbican—an outer defence of mound and ditch with two entrances like funnels.

About 56 B.C. Maiden Castle became directly involved with upheavals that were happening on the continent. During Julius Caesar's Gallic campaign he had repressed a rebellion by the Veneti tribe. Once powerful, now forced to flee to avoid slavery, many of them left Brittany for Cornwall which, as traders in tin, they already knew. Some of them landed on the Dorset coast, discovered Maiden Castle and took control of it, probably quite easily, for the people of the hill-fort had grown lackadaisical through the long years of peace.

The refugees quickly remodelled the existing defences on the lines of the forts they had known in Brittany. The main wall was made twice as high and much stronger. They added two extra lines of mounds and ditches so that invaders could not get within 140 yards of the fort on the south side, or 100 yards on the north. The newcomers were used to sling-stone warfare, and adapted Maiden Castle in this way so that they would have the advantage of being able to hurl pebbles with deadly accuracy from a leather sling before the enemy could retaliate.

The height from which the defenders were able to work was an added advantage. An attacker would have an almost impossible task trying to scale the huge ramparts.

A large store of ammunition, consisting of stones gathered from the nearby Chesil Beach, was found during the excavation—over twenty thousand stones in one hoard alone.

During the next eighty years or so the mighty citadel took the shape it has today, though the weathering of nineteen hundred years has of course softened its outlines, partly filled in the ditches, and rounded the ramparts.

The Veneti held the fort without, as far as we know, having to defend it. About A.D. 25 they were displaced by another people from the continent, the Belgae. They had settled in Kent and Sussex, but were forced to move by pressure from Cunobelinus of Colchester, a British king who was becoming increasingly powerful in the south-east. The Belgae repaired the defences of Maiden Castle, re-paved the streets, re-designed the living area within the walls, and prepared for a long stay . . .

The long, so far peaceful, story of Maiden Castle came to a violent end some time between A.D. 43 and 47. Vespasian, who later became a Roman Emperor, was at that time the commander of the Second Augustan Legion. He chose Maiden Castle as one of the twenty places he had decided to capture and subdue in his attempt to bring southern England under Roman control.

The battle with the Belgic defenders was fierce, short and bloody. Sir Mortimer Wheeler was able to reconstruct the course of the battle from the evidence found during the excavation.

The Roman artillery advanced towards the gates and went into action with a volley of iron-headed arrows from their catapults.

Under this cover the infantry moved up the slope, slashing through the ramparts until they reached the gates, outside which were a number of wooden huts. A blazing torch soon had the structures spluttering into flame. As the dense smoke rose and hid the Romans they stormed the gates and pounded into the fort.

They were met by the obstinate Belgae, who were determined to offer every kind of resistance, but had little chance against the better-armed, well-disciplined legionaries. The invaders killed everybody they could reach, hacking the bodies viciously and indiscriminately, so that women as well as men fell wounded and dying.

After the slaughter, the destruction. The gates and the stone walls on either side of them were torn down. When night came the victorious soldiers retired to their camp in the valley, well pleased with the success of their brief campaign. Another stronghold taken—another victory for Vespasian. And while they ate, drank, boasted, and finally fell asleep by their camp fires, the few Britons of Maiden Castle who had survived crept out of hiding to bury their dead.

Sir Mortimer Wheeler and his helpers found the cemetery under the ashes of the burnt-out huts outside the eastern entrance.

The graves had been dug quickly and fearfully. The bodies of twenty-three men and eleven women were brought to light. Many of the skulls had cuts in them—one had nine deep gashes in it—and all the bodies were in positions which showed that they had been buried hastily and unceremoniously; some were crouching, others were lying awkwardly on their backs or sides.

One particularly interesting find was an arrow-head deeply embedded in a vertebra of the victim's spine. When the dead had been buried, objects that would give them sustenance in the after-life—drinking-bowls, a mug, and joints of lamb—were put in the graves. Even in their grief and terror the friends and relations of the slain insisted on following tradition and paying their respects.

The present resting-place of the skeletons and their pathetic belongings is Dorchester Museum.

What happened next is supposition, but it is based on logical reasoning. The people of the hill-fort salvaged what they could out of the ruins, rebuilt as much as they were able, and tried to put together their shattered lives. They knew, however, that their independence was over, and that their future depended on the whims of their Roman overlords. And while they struggled on, they watched the walls of a new town rising up in the valley, the Roman city we now know as Dorchester.

Eventually Maiden Castle was abandoned, for the third time. What point was there in keeping on a stronghold that had lost its usefulness? The Romans did not want it; they had their own, more modern, methods of defence. So, about A.D. 75, the humans departed, and the nibbling sheep took over.

That is not quite the end of the story, though. For three hundred years Maiden Castle remained deserted, but just before the end of the Roman period in Britain a little temple was built within the eastern gate, with a priest's house next to it. About a hundred coins were found there, the latest being of the reign of Honorious, who died in A.D. 423, and this seems to prove that when the Roman rule in Britain collapsed the temple was left to fall into ruins.

Another two hundred years went by . . . and at the top

of the hill a single Saxon soldier was buried. Exactly when or why, we shall never know.

Potsherds, arrow-heads, ashes, coins, the line of a ditch, walls of chalk slabs, the gaps left when posts rotted away, stone pebbles used as ammunition, bent and mutilated skeletons, a litter of stone blocks—these are the clues that led to the intelligent and imaginative reconstruction of the long, involved story of the most imposing of all the earthworks of England.

CHAPTER TWELVE

THE PEAT BOG MYSTERY

AMONG the high hills near Aarhus, in Central Jutland, in a lonely, heather-covered valley, is a narrow peat bog called Tollund Mose. On May 8, 1950, some peat-cutters were working there. They had opened up a trench seven feet deep and were just about to dig even deeper when one of them gave a gasp and pointed at something in the hole. The others pressed closer and peered down.

Part of a body lay there in a crouched position, naked, dark-brown, shrivelled—a foot and a shoulder protruding from the soft, dark peat . . .

'Murder,' one of the men breathed. 'We have uncovered a murder. We must tell the police immediately.'

Professor Peter Glob, an archaeologist, was in the middle of a lecture at Aarhus University when he was called away to the telephone. It was the superintendent of the police station at Silkeborg who wanted to speak to him.

'Professor Glob,' the policeman said, 'can you come to Tollund Mose immediately? I have just received word that a body has been found, very well preserved, its skin dyed brown by the peat-acid. It may be a case of murder, or it may be something in your line of country. I am going to the peat bog myself now—will you meet me there?'

That morning the professor's students had to be content

with only half a lecture. At Tollund Mose, Professor Glob climbed down into the damp pit. Carefully he removed more peat from the body and exposed the head. After a swift examination he straightened up to face the impatient policeman and the silent peat-cutters.

'Yes,' he said, 'it's murder all right, but a murder that was committed perhaps two thousand years ago! Now, I shall want all you men to lift him out so that we can get him to the National Museum in Copenhagen for a proper investigation. If we delay, the air will destroy him.'

For the first time a note of excitement crept into his voice.

'This is a remarkable discovery. Many crushed and broken bodies have been found in the bogs, but never one so intact. See how he looks as though he is sleeping. Look at his expression, so peaceful and calm. One can hardly believe that he is really dead!'

The men gazed at the body. They noticed that it was not completely naked, for round the waist was a leather belt, knotted in a noose over the stomach; and on the head was a small hat made of skins, tied under the chin by a strap. The professor pointed to something else that was now visible.

'There is the cause of death,' he said, 'a leather noose drawn tightly round the neck. Our prehistoric friend was strangled . . .'

Under Professor Glob's direction they covered the body with peat again, then cut out the whole section and placed it in a wooden case. The mystery man began his journey to Copenhagen.

At the laboratory of the National Museum examination and research began straight away. It was reluctantly decided that to keep the whole body would be too difficult, so only the head and feet were submitted to the long treatment that would preserve them permanently. The rest of the body was given a post-mortem.

To see the head of Tollund Man in the Silkeborg Museum,

where it is now kept, is an awe-inspiring experience. It is like going back in time to meet prehistoric man in the flesh —a man who is going to wake up at any moment, open his eyes and *live*.

Head of Tollund Man

It is not the face of a stranger. There is nothing savage about it. One could meet men with similar faces anywhere in the western world. Now it is slightly smaller than it was in life because preservation has caused it to shrink.

It is black and looks like polished leather. The features are clear-cut and noble; there are wrinkles at the corners of the eyes, and stubble on his chin. Normally he would have been clean-shaven, but the hair continued to grow a little after death. He looks as though he was a wise man and knew how to smile. His expression is enigmatic but peaceful, suggesting that he died willingly, without a struggle, ready to meet his fate.

Who was he? Why was he put to death in that fashion? What is the significance of the burial? Without being able to give absolutely certain answers to those questions, enough is known about life in Denmark's Iron Age to make shrewd deductions.

Some of the possibilities can be dismissed out of hand. It is hardly likely that a man who had committed suicide by hanging himself from a tree would have been carefully cut down and buried in that way, with the rope still round his neck. Nor is it likely that he was murdered by an enemy. The body had no marks of violence on it, and in the faraway time when Tollund Man lived a club rather than a rope was the usual weapon.

Perhaps the man with the wise face had been hanged because he was a criminal whose actions had outraged the tribal code. Or he might have been a prisoner of war who became useless to his captors. But surely in either of those cases he would have been thrown into the bog casually, without the preliminary hanging, which was, strangely enough, an honourable, even sacred, form of death.

And there we have a clue to the most likely reason for Tollund Man being where he was, and in the condition he was; that he had been the central figure in a tribal rite that included a sacrificial hanging.

In Iron Age times in Denmark some naked hangings were connected with a spring festival which was designed to placate the dark gods and ensure a fruitful harvest. Others took place at the death of the year, the winter solstice. Winter or spring, Tollund Man, who was perhaps the headman of a settlement, had volunteered to bring fertility and good fortune in a time of scarcity by offering himself to the gods in a solemn ceremony of chants and dancing which culminated in the moment when the noose was pulled tight about his neck . . . Then his body would be placed where all sacrificial offerings to the gods were taken—in the peat bog.

The contents of Tollund Man's stomach offer some evidence in support of the theory of sacrifice. His last meal, eaten during the twenty-four hours before his death, was entirely vegetable. There were no traces of meat at all. It had been a kind of porridge consisting of barley, linseed, camelina—or 'gold of pleasure', which is a member of the mustard family—and pale persicaria, a plant which grows on waste ground. In addition, and probably included by accident, were small quantities of the seeds of wild plants such as sheep's sorrel, white goosefoot from the turnip family, corn spurrey and wild pansy. The ingredients would have been boiled together, perhaps with honey to make them more tasty, or with salt if the victim did not have a sweet tooth.

Were the times so severe that men were forced to eat such concoctions as part of their daily diet? We know that game was scarce, but domestic animals were kept—though perhaps they were only eaten on special occasions. Or was the porridge of mixed seeds a ritual meal, eaten to symbolize the fruits of the earth that the invisible powers would graciously permit to flourish after a sacrifice had been made to them?

Tollund Man will always remain a mystery, and perhaps it is better so. The romantic imaginings that have resulted from a study of that haunting face would quickly give way to embarrassment if it turned out that the owner had been a notorious criminal, put to death for stealing sheep!

CHAPTER THIRTEEN

DEATH IN THE MORNING

THE day dawned bright and hot in the Italian city of Pompeii, situated a few miles south of Naples and five miles south-east of Vesuvius. It was hot, too, in the quiet little fishing town of Herculaneum on the coast, which was also overshadowed by the sleeping volcano.

'Another day of unbearable heat,' yawned the earliest risers, the slaves, shopkeepers and farm workers. They did not realize just how true their words were . . .

Half-way through that morning of August 24, in the year A.D. 79, a staggering, deafening crack like the noise of a thousand thunderstorms suddenly split the air over Pompeii. At the same time the ground started to tremble as though in the grip of an uncontrollable ague.

Something put a mighty hand over the sun's face, and an eerie darkness took its place. Birds fell from the sky, stricken in mid-flight, and from the earth heat rose in burning, searing blasts.

The daily life of all the flourishing towns and villages in the region round Vesuvius stopped.

Terrified people dropped their cooking-pots, left their dinners on the table, and abandoned their lathes and forges, their tools, books and money transactions. The men rushed out of the wine-shops and public baths. The women's gossip about children, clothes and high prices came to an abrupt end. A funeral stopped in mid-procession. Prisoners strained against their stocks. Dogs howled, pulling at their chains. Priests offering sacrifices in the temple left their sacred vessels. Crowds gathered in the streets and market-place and gazed around.

'What has happened?'

'Is this a visitation from the gods?'

'What have we done that they are angry with us?'

Then all eyes turned towards Vesuvius, the great volcano that had been reasonably calm and peaceful for so long. There were gasps of horror. The mountain had changed its shape!

The rounded summit had split open, and out of the gaping mouth mushroom-shaped clouds of smoke and tongues of flame were being thrown up into the sky. White-hot stones hurtled through the air like a continuous shower of shooting stars gone mad.

Volcanic ash, turned by rain to burning mud, was pouring from the rim of the crater and rolling down the mountain slopes, licking at everything in its path and curling long arms like an enormous octopus. The walls of country villas swayed and fell before its inexorable advance, and farm-land disappeared under the grey flood. Trees bent groaning before it, then snapped, and animals struggled for a moment before they too were engulfed. The avalanche reached Herculaneum, and quickly flowed through the streets, into the houses, through the windows, and settled over everything like thick treacle.

Then the vomit from the volcano rushed towards the boiling, heaving water of the sea, and with an angry roar met the waves headlong. In some places the waves crashed forward, striking at harbours, crushing galleons and breaking up pleasure craft into splinters. Elsewhere the mud forced the sea back, exposing to the burning darkness sea creatures that had never before left the safety of deep waters.

113

There had been an earthquake in A.D. 62, but its effects had been nothing like this.

In Pompeii, on the other side of the mountain from the

The ruins of Pompeii

sea, panic swept over the inhabitants. They were assaulted by a rain of grey ash and bombarded by pebbles and boulders which crashed down on them like hail. Sulphur gas caught at their throats and made them retch. Their eyes watered; they staggered about, coughing and blinded, seeking vainly for shelter. They shuttered their windows and crouched in corners, covering their heads, or they stumbled out into the open.

There was no escape. Wherever they tried to hide they choked to death—men, women, children, dogs, birds . . . Rooftops crashed on some of them, and walls tumbled about them. Scorching cinders set fire to furniture and clothes. Metal dissolved, and solid objects were swept away as easily as a child knocks down his wooden bricks.

Prayers to the gods were useless, even if there had been time to pray. Some people managed to load carts with as many valuables as they could hurriedly pack, and many of them got through the gates safely. But others were not so lucky. The carts piled up in the streets at the city gates and caused a great traffic jam, and soon it was impossible to move in any direction.

Every town and village within a radius of about fifteen miles from Vesuvius suffered in the disaster. Herculaneum disappeared under thousands of tons of molten lava. At Pompeii a layer of grey ash and stones settled silently over everything, thickening and hardening until the city was buried twenty feet below it. One day there was a bustling, prosperous little town of, perhaps, twenty thousand inhabitants. Within twenty-four hours there was nothing to be seen but what looked like drifts of dirty snow covering two thousand of them.

The following day the sun appeared from behind its pall and shone on utter desolation. Thin wisps of smoke were the only indication that something unusual had happened inside the volcano. In the hills above the dead towns the people who had escaped wandered about, dazed with shock, hardly realizing that they would never see their homes and families again.

The world soon forgot the tragedy of Pompeii and Herculaneum. Hundreds of years slid by. Legends persisted for a time, but they were confused and vague. Barbarians overran Italy, and at different times Saracens, Germans and Spaniards fought there. Vesuvius, apparently exhausted by the violence of its outburst, slept on through the centuries. Villages and small towns appeared on its slopes, and gardens, woods and vineyards grew. On the ground beneath which Herculaneum was hidden a city called Resina was built.

One day in 1710, a peasant of Resina, while deepening his dried-up well to find another source of water, found some blocks of marble in the rocky earth. When the news of the find reached an Austrian colonel who was planning to build a splendid country house near by he went to see it for himself. He realized that the pieces of marble must have come from a building now deep underground. He promptly bought the peasant's land and started his own excavations.

With the well as a starting-point tunnels were bored through the ruins of Herculaneum with complete disregard for what might be destroyed. The statues, vases and candelabra that the workmen found went straight to the colonel's villa. When the theatre, which is what by chance the excavators had lighted upon, had been denuded of its treasures the colonel lost interest. It was spoil he was after. He had no interest in exploring the past for its own sake.

So Herculaneum sank back into oblivion. In 1738 King Charles III of Naples became interested in the possibility of further finds. Fresh excavations, directed in a very haphazard way by a Spanish military engineer, yielded bronze statues of men on horseback, jewels, weapons, coins, and an inscribed stone that positively identified the town and the theatre.

But digging into the tons of solidified lava was hard work, and it was decided to transfer operations to the other side of the mountain just in case anything might turn up there. In 1748 the walls of a house covered with paintings were found, and the bones of a man who had died while trying to escape. In his hands were some coins—all he had been able to grab as he fled.

Gradually the excavators became interested in things other

than the art treasures that were filling the king's museum. The Great Theatre of Pompeii was laid bare in 1764, and in the years that followed the barracks of the gladiators, the Temple of Isis and the Villa of Diomedes. The workmen did not, as before, stop digging when it seemed to be leading nowhere, but carried on regardless of what might or might not turn up.

There were interruptions to the work, though. Vesuvius must have resented the discovery of its former wickedness. Several times in the early part of the eighteenth century it awoke with ominous rumblings and spittings. In 1759 it erupted with serious consequences.

Early in the nineteenth century, after a French conquest of Italy, Joseph Bonaparte, brother of the more famous Napoleon, ordered his engineers to organize the digging up of Pompeii more efficiently. A later king of Naples was inspired to plan the restoration of the city as well as its clearance. He declared that he would, as far as possible, make it look as it did before the great catastrophe. A labour force of five hundred got to work, and the streets, houses, temples, shops and theatres began to rise out of the rubbish. Skeletons, unfortunately, crumbled into dust as soon as they were exposed to the air, for no one knew how to preserve them.

The technique of excavation at Pompeii became really scientific when a distinguished archaeologist named Giuseppe Fiorelli took charge in 1860. He brought to the task great talent, determination and enthusiasm. He started a journal of the excavation, and it was much more business-like than the former gossipy diary which had recorded little but the visits of important people to the site.

Whatever Fiorelli found was described in detail and classified; its position on the site and its relation to other objects were carefully measured. It was the kind of recording that nowadays is done by photography.

Fiorelli's work started at the beginning of the 'golden age of archaeology'. Science was making great strides, and he was able to take advantage of new processes and methods. Also he could compare his results with those of other archaeologists who were busy in other parts of the world.

Since Fiorelli's time excavations have gone on almost without interruption. Italian archaeologists are still at work at Pompeii. Now more than three-fifths of the city have been uncovered and restored, and new finds are constantly being made.

If you visit Pompeii today you can see some of it much as its inhabitants saw it before it disappeared overnight. Damaged woodwork has been replaced, roofs and balconies rebuilt. Statues, mosaics and frescoes illustrating Greek myths or everyday occupations have been returned to their original positions in the sumptuous villas. You can walk along the four main highways which led to the eight gates in the city walls, one of which was found in 1954. You can stand in the main square or wander into the inns, snack bars and wine-shops which border the traffic-rutted streets on high pavements. (Money left on the tables as the customers made a hurried exit is still there.) You can pass under the three great archways, examine the water-heating system of the public baths, and read (if you know Latin) the many election notices, the houses-to-let advertisements, and what was on at the theatres and sports arena.

On the walls of shops and inns, both inside and out, are hundreds of stylus-scrawled comments. Some of the writing is extremely vulgar—and amusing too. You can visit the cellar containing the twenty people who vainly sought shelter there. You can see a bowl of eggs on a kitchen table, a batch of loaves like large hot-cross buns (now carbonized) in a baker's oven, a set of surgical instruments, the wax tablets of a banker, the remains of a dog on its leash, the fuller's dye vats, the olive press at the oil merchant's and the corn-mill at the baker's (both still workable); and hundreds of other articles which bring to life the intimate details of the busy lives of the white-toga'd ghosts who walk unseen by your side, whose vigorous activities were brought to a sudden, permanent halt.

For the archaeologist Pompeii and Herculaneum have been godsends. Other ancient cities have been sacked, razed to the ground, or have died slowly and quietly over a period of time. Archaeologists have had to reconstruct them from a few fragments of pots, corroded metal, decomposed materials and disjointed bones, or by deciphering inscriptions in unknown languages. But in Pompeii everything was there, just waiting to be uncovered; and the writings were in Latin, easy to read.

It requires no effort of imagination to bring the dead city to life. Contact with the past is immediate. And what is most important is that it is not with kings, tyrants or empire-builders that one becomes involved, but with the common people—the tradesman, dancing-girl, gladiator, the lovesick young man, drunkard and child. Everybody, luckily, could read and write, and most of them did—on walls!

CHAPTER FOURTEEN

TEMPLE FROM THE RUBBLE

ON April 10, 1954, *The Times* carried a small item of news:

'Excavations at Walbrook were reported yesterday to have revealed further fragments from Roman London. An almost complete section of a wall has been uncovered, disclosing a large square piece of masonry which might have been an altar.'

This modest paragraph, tucked away at the bottom of page 8, contained no hint that a 'nine-days wonder' was about to happen, or that the people of London would soon be roused to a pitch of excitement rarely equalled in the history of archaeological research. No one foresaw that Government ministers would become involved, that experts would write letters to the papers and argue fiercely with each other, or that the police would have to deal with angry crowds!

Yet all those things happened. Here first is the background to the story.

During the Second World War vast areas of the City of London were reduced to rubble by German bombs, and when the war was over an immense programme of rebuilding was begun. The misfortunes of war turned into good fortune for archaeologists. Here at last, they decided, was an opportunity to investigate as thoroughly as possible, and for as long as time would allow, the area of devastation in the City, in the midst of which only St Paul's seemed to stand unharmed. So in 1947 the London Roman and Medieval Excavation Council was formed, financed by private subscription and a grant from the Ministry of Works; and excavations started.

In the Walbrook area the main object was to discover the position of the bed of the River Walbrook which had, in Roman times, flowed through a valley which today lies between St Paul's to the west and Cornhill to the east, and was supposed to follow more or less the course of Walbrook, the street which bears its name. On Roman maps the stream is shown as a broad channel about 45 feet wide, fed by a number of tributaries; and it was thought that it was once wide and deep enough to enable quite large craft to sail along it as far as where the Bank of England now stands.

The eastern part of Walbrook had been effectively bulldozed in 1949 before new offices were built, a method which *The Times* observed tartly 'did not lend itself to accurate recording of the results'. In the western area the digging was supervised by Mr W. F. Grimes, then the Director of the London Museum, now the Professor of Archaeology at London University, and a very experienced excavator.

He started in 1952, in the cellar of a bombed building that was less choked with rubble than the rest of the site. Very early in the proceedings he discovered the presence of some kind of Roman building, though exactly what it was was not at first clear. When half of it had been exposed it was seen to be basilican in form: that is, it was a large, oblong building with an apse at one end, a nave, and side aisles separated by two groups of seven pillars.

Another fact soon became apparent. The course of the Walbrook stream did *not* follow the line of the street, as had been thought, because the building which was being

121

slowly cleared cut across that line. Therefore the river must have flowed either to the east or to the west of the building. Mr Grimes reasoned that the west was the more likely position so, postponing further work on the building itself, he cut more trenches to the west of the apse.

Months of hard work followed, during which the diggers worked under great difficulties due to the flooding of the trenches, and sometimes they were knee-deep in water. In spite of this, a fairly complete picture of this part of the Walbrook valley was obtained.

The result of the operations showed that the river was only about 14 feet wide, and that it was very shallow, for its bed was only between 32 and 35 feet below the present-day street level. The great river capable of taking the largest ships the Romans could build had, after all, been a modest stream lined with retaining walls made from wooden planks.

Early in 1954, when work on the River Walbrook was in full swing, the builders announced that they were ready to begin laying the foundations of the fourteen-storey block of offices which was to rise on the site. There was still a great amount of work to be done by the excavators, and the Roman building had hardly begun to yield up its secrets. Would there be time to discover anything more about it?

When the builders' machines and implements appeared on the site things became really urgent. Yet how could Mr Grimes and his small team of helpers move the tons of rubble and earth which covered the area under which the rest of the building probably lay? The first of many turning points came when the owners of the site helpfully set their men to clear away the debris which was holding the excavators back.

As more of the building came to light Mr Grimes was able to make a complete plan of it. He came to the conclusion that it was a Roman temple dedicated to Mithras, a god worshipped seventeen hundred years ago, when it was touch and go whether Mithraism or Christianity would gain the ascendancy in the west.

The estimated date for the original temple was the late second century A.D., although alterations had been made at various times until the fourth century. Some time in the fourth century the temple had fallen into disuse.

Before the interest of Londoners was dramatically aroused, Mr Grimes's theory that the temple was associated with Mithras was confirmed. The lower part of a limestone figure holding a lighted torch pointing downward was found near the south wall. It was identified as that of Cautopates, who represented Darkness and Night and was one of Mithras's two attendants. The other member of the trinity was Cautes who, with torch held aloft, represented Day.

A slab showing Mithras slaying a bull had already been found in the Walbrook area in 1896, and is now in the London Museum. Writing in 1902, Franz Cumont, a great expert on Mithraism, observed, 'The existence of a mithraeum in London should not surprise us.' It had only taken fifty years for us not to be surprised!

It was a bitter blow to Mr Grimes and his colleagues that, because of the pressing need to start on the foundations of Bucklersbury House, they could not continue their work. They had, however, a lot to be thankful for. The willingness of the builders to assist with the back-breaking job of clearing the site had been an immense help, and that so much of the temple had been revealed was due to that help. But now, it seemed, the end had come. On the following Monday, September 20, the bulldozers would crash their way through the site and everything would be crushed under them . . .

The deadline approached. A reprieve seemed impossible. Then, three days before the hour of doom, a spark that was to set off a great controversy was struck by a newspaper reporter in search of a week-end story. He happened to be passing the site, went on to it and spoke to some of the people who were still digging feverishly.

He probably did not expect to get much of a story from a lot of technical details, but he was mistaken. The archaeologists spoke freely and feelingly to him. After all, it could do no harm. By the time the public knew about the temple it would be nothing more than a memory—a carefully plotted and photographed memory, but soon it would lie even more hidden, this time under a giant building, than when it had been only a few feet under the earth.

As the reporter listened to them and watched their last desperate efforts to uncover the remains he realized that he had got a first-rate story, one which no other paper had the slightest inkling of. He rushed back to his office, knocked the story into shape and had his copy ready in time for Saturday's paper. Saturday, the day before the last day . . .

That one story was sufficient to awaken the pride of Londoners in their city and their respect for its past. There is usually a lull in the activities of the City on Saturdays, so the workers on the building site were surprised to see the crowds arrive, at first in their dozens, and then in hundreds.

What had made them come? Was it curiosity, sentiment, or a genuine love of antiquities? It was probably a mixture of all those things, plus a deep-down need to identify themselves with their city, with its two thousand years' history, after a war which had threatened its existence. Although they might not put it into words, perhaps they sensed that the past demanded as much respect as the present and the future.

It was a wonderful moment in London's history and, as if to emphasize the fact, a strange coincidence played a part in the drama.

Later in the day, with sightseers clambering all over the site looking for souvenirs, and reporters and photographers scribbling and clicking away like mad, the marble head of Mithras himself, corroded and discoloured by time, was lifted out of its long resting-place at the eastern end of the temple!

It was indescribably beautiful. Perched on the top was

a Phrygian cap like a cone with the peak bent in the front.
(That alone identified the head with the Mithraic cult.) The
wide eyes seemed to be looking up to the sky. The nose was

Marble head of Mithras

straight and beautifully modelled. The full lips were slightly
parted. At the eleventh hour the god had revealed himself—
his last appearance before the destruction of his temple!
The Sunday Press headlined the story and the likely fate

of the temple. The hundreds of visitors became thousands—and the bulldozers stood by menacingly, ready to go into action the next day . . .

The Times reported on Monday morning that several people had called at their office to protest. But there was little hope of a reprieve. The position of the temple made it impossible for it to be preserved where it was, because it lay in the middle of what would be the basement of the new building. The archaeologists were not keen for it to be removed to another site because, they argued, that would destroy its significance. Nevertheless, the public was very angry indeed. Sensing the mood of the people, the newspapers were angry too.

Monday's *Times* also had a leading article on the subject, headed A TEMPLE FOR DESTRUCTION?

'The excavation,' it said, 'is still far from complete, and it seems that it will never be completed. Within a matter of hours from the writing of these words, the whole structure, with anything else that may be hidden under adjoining parts of the site, is apparently to be bulldozed out of existence . . .'

Other papers had joined the protest, and the whole city bristled with indignation. The owners of the site, and the contractors, who had already gone to a great deal of trouble and expense to help the excavators, must have smarted under the implication that they were without conscience and wanted to break up the temple just for the fun of it.

Fortunately *The Times* leader was read by the Minister of Works, Sir David (now Lord) Eccles. He, Sir Harold Emmerson, Permanent Secretary to the Minister of Works, and Mr Charlton of the Department of Ancient Monuments, visited the site, and they were impressed with what they saw. They consulted the owners immediately, and the clearing away was postponed.

The bulldozers went to work, but they were instructed to keep away from the temple. The excavators were given until the next week-end. Mr Grimes and his team heaved sighs of relief and went on digging . . .

Sir David Eccles held little hope of preserving the temple where it stood '. . . in the middle of a building site,' he said, 'for which there has been issued a building licence for £2,750,000.'

Then Mr Grimes made a statement that was later misunderstood.

'We have a complete record of the finds and the materials,' he said. 'That is the scientific information which interests archaeologists, and the actual preservation is a secondary thing.'

Mr Grimes was indebted to the owners, the Legenland Trust, who had made the excavation possible. He was anxious to keep faith with the firm and to avoid involving it in further heavy financial loss. He also realized that it would be disastrous if, because of the Legenland Trust's experience, other firms were reluctant to co-operate with archaeologists in the future.

During the next few days *The Times* carried a flood of letters. One was from Mr A. V. Bridgland of the Legenland Trust, trying to clear up any misunderstanding. He said that his company had borne the cost of nearly two years of excavations, and explained that it was out of the question to consider making an arch over the temple to support part of the office block. The subsoil was unstable, and thousands of piles would be needed to carry the new building, even according to present plans.

On September 21 the contractors announced that the public could visit the temple officially between 5.30 p.m. and 6.30 p.m. for the next five days. Barriers were put up and the City police prepared to deal with the crowds. Thousands of people decided to see for themselves what all the fuss was about.

They started queueing at 4 o'clock, and by 5.30 the queue stretched right round the site, growing steadily longer as people finished work and joined it. Even when the closing

E 127

time was extended to 7 p.m. hundreds were disappointed at being unable to get near the centre of the excitement. There were complaints and arguments, and even scuffles with the police as angry people were turned away.

It was on that day that the neck and throat belonging to the Mithras head were found, and the pieces fitted together perfectly . . .

Sir David Eccles made a report on the situation to the Prime Minister, Mr (later Sir) Winston Churchill, in which he held out little hope of the temple being allowed to stay where it was. The instability of the ground was one of the reasons he quoted, but the main difficulty was that if the temple was scheduled as an ancient monument the Government would have to pay a huge sum in compensation to the owners of the site.

Money seemed to be at the root of all the trouble. It seemed that the Government did not care whose money was involved as long as it wasn't the Government's! Sir David Eccles was reported as saying that he did not think it would be worth while having the remains re-erected elsewhere.

This made people ask—worth while for whom? It would certainly be worth while for archaeologists, and for the thousands of sightseers representing many thousands more who *cared* what happened to this remarkable piece of London's history.

The next day the queue was so long that anybody joining the end at 5.30, when the barriers were lifted, would be the last to enter at closing time.

Meanwhile, the big guns of the archaeology world were firing their shots in the correspondence columns of newspapers. Sir Mortimer Wheeler wrote to say that he considered that the pace of excavations of the areas laid waste by bombing had been too leisurely, and that a few archaeologists tackling such an immense task was like attacking a battleship with a pea-shooter. He brushed aside all the technical excuses. He had no doubt that the proper solution would be to keep the temple under Bucklersbury House.

Another correspondent made the sarcastic comment that if the site had contained 'nationalized coal or oil' further building would have stopped immediately. Someone else calculated that the cost of preservation would be re-couped in thirty-five to forty years by admission fees alone.

Professor Toynbee allied himself with Sir Mortimer Wheeler and the other people who thought that preservation was important. He put into words what thousands of people were thinking—that the most detailed reports were no substitute for the thing itself, this building which had echoed to the voices of Roman soldiers and had witnessed the strange rituals of the Mithraic priests.

One of the most startling moments of the whole operation happened on the evening of September 26.

Mr Grimes and his team, now assisted by extra volunteers, had been digging carefully all day. One of the assistants was Mr Norman Cook, Keeper of the Guildhall Museum, into whose charge the marvellous discoveries were eventually placed. The now familiar crowd of sightseers was slowly passing the temple and, as usual, more people were waiting patiently outside for their turn to enter. The September dusk was falling and very soon work would have to stop for the day.

Suddenly there was a quickening of excitement among the excavators which at once communicated itself to the sightseers. Mrs Audrey Williamson, Mr Grimes's assistant, had been digging in the part of the temple where Mithras's head had been found. Brushing away the soil from something hard which was protruding from the ground, she felt the cold smoothness of marble. Gingerly she eased it out of the earth and lifted it up with trembling hands. It was not another part of the Mithras statue, which would not have been unexpected, but another head altogether!

The excavators gathered round it in the dying light. There was a murmur from the onlookers, wondering what had happened. It was a moving moment, one that Mr Grimes wanted to share with all those present. He asked Mr Cook to hold the head up for everybody to see. He did so, not only to the fortunate people on the site, but also to those waiting beyond the barrier.

There was an awe-struck silence as they looked on the classical features of Minerva, her curled hair surmounted by part of what was probably a helmet. This was the first time for nearly two thousand years that she had been seen by human eyes. At that moment every single person present felt as though he had a personal stake in the temple and all it had revealed. How *could* they permit its destruction?

But the question other people were asking was, how *can* it possibly be preserved?

Representatives of the Ministry of Works and of the owners, led by Sir David Eccles and Mr Bridgland, met and discussed the next move. It would cost £500,000 to keep the temple where it was, £100,000 of it for making a bridge over the temple, and £400,000 to cover the loss that would result in reducing the height of Bucklersbury House (for a bridge could not support more than two storeys), and for the delay in completing the building.

'The Ministry,' said a report, 'are considering these figures . . .'

But it was pretty clear to everybody that the temple was doomed. Half a million pounds is a large sum by any standards . . .

By the end of the month the public were no longer admitted to the site, though excavating continued. City workers presented a petition to the Lord Mayor, but there seemed to be little more that anyone could do.

Then, on October 2, *The Times* announced joyfully that the remains of the Temple of Mithras were to be preserved!

This was a shock, though a pleasant one. What had happened to make the Government change its mind? Well, what had *not* happened was a sudden uprush of generosity from the Ministry of Works. It was Mr Bridgland and the Legenland Trust who turned out to be the 'heroes'. In

130

addition to all the expense they had already borne, they were willing to pay out another £10,000 to move the temple about eighty yards away to the eastern side of the forecourt of Bucklersbury House in Queen Victoria Street.

It was a compromise solution but clearly, in the circumstances, the only one possible.

Sir David Eccles presented his report and the owners' offer to the Prime Minister at a Cabinet meeting, and it was accepted with eagerness. It would have been surprising if it had not been. Everybody, or nearly everybody, satisfied, and not a penny to pay out of public funds. What could have been better!

The temple now stands in Queen Victoria Street between Bucklersbury House and Temple Court. Among the modern buildings which tower above it it is still an impressive and moving sight.

The treasures of the temple were on display in the Guildhall Museum (housed in the Royal Exchange) until the end of 1967, when they were moved, together with other collections, to new premises near Basinghall Street. A collection of replicas and photographs can be seen in the Walbrook entrance of Bucklersbury House, which was built over the exact spot where the temple stood. Over the office doors there are glass panels exquisitely engraved with characters and symbols of Mithraism.

That so much of London's mithraeum can be seen is due to Mr Grimes and his devoted helpers; to Mr Bridgland and the Legenland Trust, who footed so many bills and behaved with such understanding; and to the Press and people of London whose agitations and protests did not fall on deaf ears.

CHAPTER FIFTEEN

GHOST SHIP

IN the year A.D. 655 a king of East Anglia died fighting in distant Yorkshire. Whether he was killed by a spear or drowned in winter floods we do not know. But his body was never seen again in his native Suffolk, and his people mourned him as a hero.

The king's name was Aethelhere. He had given up the new religion that was sweeping the country—for, by the middle of the seventh century, most of Britain was a Christian country—and he had turned back to the pagan gods of the Norsemen.

Aethelhere had only reigned for a year before he was killed. When the news from Yorkshire at last reached Suffolk, Aethelwald, the dead king's brother and now the new king, felt that he must honour Aethelhere's memory by building a public monument to him.

Aethelwald had to decide whether the monument should be Christian or pagan. Being a Christian, he would have preferred the former, but he wondered whether his brother, journeying to a new life in Valhalla, would be happy to know that his treasures were lying in a Christian grave. Aethelhere had been an enemy of the new religion after he had rejected it. Indeed, his wife had left him to become a nun because he opposed her conversion, and he had allied himself with Penda, the pagan King of Mercia, against the Christian King of Northumbria. So Aethelwald reluctantly chose the pagan rite of ship burial as his brother's cenotaph.

On a bleak winter's day early in 656 a large number of Saxon labourers hauled a heavy wooden clinker-built ship from the estuary of the River Deben, and pulled it, bow first, half a mile inland and then up a steep hill to the burial ground of Aethelhere's family. A huge trench, not less than a hundred feet long, twenty feet wide and ten feet deep, which had been dug out of the sandy soil, was waiting to receive the ship. Wooden rollers had been placed over the trench, and the sweating, straining men pushed the ship forward till it was resting on them.

They passed ropes under it and then over a series of thick posts set in the ground on either side of the hole. When the ropes were holding the ship firm the rollers were carefully withdrawn, the ropes were slowly lowered, and the ship sank neatly into its grave, almost filling the whole space. All the deck-work and seating were taken out, and only the ribs were left.

Aethelwald had brought to the grave all the things his brother would need during his journey to the after-life, and supplies for when he arrived. These were solemnly laid amidships and then covered with bracken. They were the things a king would use when he was alive, and were therefore fitting for his death—domestic utensils, personal ornaments and weapons, and royal regalia.

Wood-cutters and carpenters next came on the scene, and they built a wooden cabin, about seventeen feet long, and with a gabled roof, over the magnificent gravegoods, which were glinting their last in the pale winter sun.

Then the cenotaph was almost complete, but there were rituals to observe before the ceremony was over. The dead king's family, his nobles and warrior friends, walked round the burial place in procession, chanting their sorrow, telling the bare ground and the salt-laden wind that a mighty man had gone to join his ancestors . . .

Workmen shovelled the sand back into the space between the ship and the sides of the trench, and over the ship itself, until there was nothing to see but a large oblong patch of newly exposed ground. When the ship was completely hidden, a huge oval mound, made of soil and tons of turf cut from the surrounding heathland, was piled up over the tomb.

Then the mourners went away, leaving the gold under the dust.

For thirteen hundred years the grave-goods of the Saxon king lay undisturbed. Aethelhere became no more than a mention in the history book of Bede. No one suspected what lay so near the surface of the turf and bracken-covered heath at Sutton Hoo, starred with tiny flowers and blown on by the four winds.

Only once, in either the sixteenth or the early seventeenth century, had grave-robbers turned their attention to the great barrow. They had sunk a shaft in what they thought was the centre of the mound but, fortunately for future excavators, wasn't. They had become discouraged before they reached any of the burial deposit. They had eaten meat and drunk wine at the bottom of the hole they had made, and then had climbed out and gone home, leaving behind them the remains of a fire, some animal bones, and a piece of broken jug.

How true the story of Aethelhere is, nobody can say for certain. But even if some of the details may be questioned we know enough about the burial customs of the Anglo-Saxons to be able to re-create in broad outline the ceremony of the last rites. What *is* certain is that a rich and important king, probably Aethelhere, was commemorated by an elaborate ship burial soon after the middle of the seventh century.

The story now jumps to 1938, when Mrs E. M. Pretty, the owner of Sutton Hoo, an estate near Woodbridge and six miles from the Suffolk sea-coast, became interested in a group of eleven barrows on her land, and made arrangements for some of them to be investigated. Mr Guy Maynard, the Curator of the Ipswich Museum, directed the operations. Mr Basil Brown was the foreman in charge of the digging.

Three barrows were opened, but the results were disappointing. One contained nothing. It had obviously been plundered. In the second barrow traces of an eighteen-feet-long clinker-built boat were found, and also evidence of a cremated body. The third barrow contained the remains of a wooden tray on which were the ashes of two cremations. It was all rather an anticlimax. After the third barrow had been opened, no further work was done.

The following year Mr Maynard suggested that he and Mr Brown should tackle another barrow. Mrs Pretty agreed. The one they chose was the largest of the eleven. It was an oblong-shaped mound, about nine feet high, and it had slumped out of shape at the western end.

In April 1939 the excavators and their helpers went to work with great caution. The rotted turf of the mound was dug away to ground level, after a slicing operation had revealed a number of rusty iron nails in such a position that they could only have held planks of wood together. In the damp sand there were patches of discoloration—all that remained of the wood itself. All the sand that had fallen into the trench and was packed round the sides could be detected because it was lighter and yellower than the stained part.

With infinite care much of it was removed. In the centre of the trench were some pieces of bronze and iron.

The excavators stopped work, aware that they were on the threshold of an immensely important discovery. A visit from Mr C. W. Phillips, now the Archaeology Officer to the Ordnance Survey, who suggested that it would be wise to get advice from other experts, led to the British Museum and the Ministry of Works being consulted. So in July an enlarged team started again.

Mr Phillips was the Director. Among his assistants were Mr (later Professor) W. F. Grimes, Professor Stuart Piggott and his wife, and Professor J. B. Ward-Perkins, now the Director of the British School at Rome. A complete record of the work was made in photographs taken by a team led by the late Dr O. G. S. Crawford.

The excavation, which was fortunately helped by an unusually windless and rainless summer, called for patience, care and extreme delicacy. The task of searching for changes in colour in the sand that would reveal the outline of the eighty-nine-feet-long ship was most exacting. Such ordinary tools were used, too: broad-bladed knives, spoons, shovels, trowels, paint-brushes, and a blunt bodkin! Moss from a nearby wood was used for packing purposes.

Mrs Pretty's gardeners did the heavy digging. The excavators were wryly amused when the Ministry of Works sent along a dozen scaffold poles and a tarpaulin—none of which was any use. Having exhausted itself by its effort, the Ministry showed no more interest in what was going on . . .

When all the sand had been removed, almost grain by grain, the plan of the ship was laid bare. The size and shape of the burial chamber, which had collapsed under the weight of sand and turf above it, could be traced by the lines of stain which crossed the ship just over seventeen feet apart. Then it was seen that the ship had really been a huge rowing-boat, perhaps used originally in the invasion of Britain by the Norsemen. Thirty-eight sailors had rowed it over the grey northern seas, with one man in the stern to steer it with a large paddle. Now it was like a ghost ship; only the outline of its shape was left to tell its story.

Finding the ship was thrilling enough, but what appeared as the sand was brushed away fulfilled the team's wildest hopes—treasure that made the contents of all other Saxon graves found previously pale into insignificance. Not that most of the objects *looked* rich and brilliant; but among the rusty, corroded lumps the yellow gleam of gold and the red glow of garnets hinted at the glories that were to come.

How to get them out of the trench without treading on other, still hidden objects was a problem. There was no overhead gantry with a travelling cradle handy! The excavators just had to tread very, very carefully. Before any of the precious articles were removed—some of them had been crushed and broken by the collapsing cabin—they were photographed in position, and drawings and notes were made so that there would be a permanent record. The site was guarded by police every night when the news got around that something extraordinary was happening at Sutton Hoo.

On August 14, 1939, a Coroner's inquest was held in the village hall at Sutton to determine whether the objects were Treasure Trove. If so, they would belong to the Crown. If gold and silver, or articles made from those metals, are buried with the intention that they should be recovered later, and if the legal owner cannot be found, then the Crown becomes the owner, though the finder is paid the market value of his find. But if such treasures are not buried in secret, and if the person who buried them intended them to stay in that place—a royal grave, for instance, a sacred lake or a holy well—then the ground landlord is declared the owner, and the Crown gives up any claim.

The Sutton Hoo treasure was returned under armed escort from the British Museum, where it had been sent, and was exhibited in the hall where the inquest took place. During the proceedings the jury heard evidence from Mrs Pretty, Mr Maynard, Mr Brown, Professor Piggott and Mr Phillips. The spectators in the crowded little hall listened spellbound to Mr Phillips's imagined reconstruction of the burial of the ship and the building of the barrow.

The jury retired. They returned once to ask for advice on the question of secrecy, but in the end their verdict was—not Treasure Trove. Whoever had buried the treasure had done it openly and had meant it to stay buried for ever. So the gold and silver belonged to Mrs Pretty; and she, a

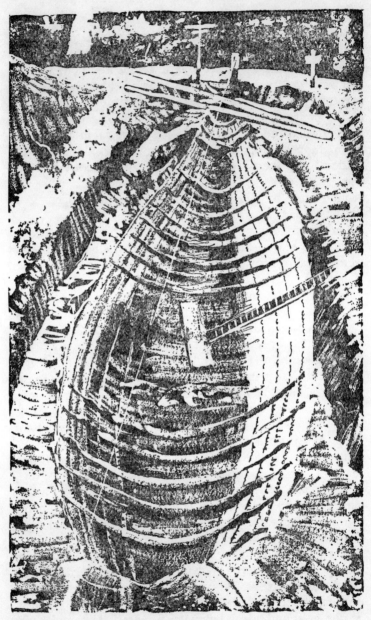

The 'ghost ship' revealed

week later, generously gave the whole of the find to the nation, to be kept at the British Museum.

All this happened at a time of great tension in the country. War was imminent, and preparations for defence against air attack were being hastily made. The excavators had just time to finish work on the site, and at the British Museum first aid was given to the articles that needed it most. Then everything was removed to a place of safety—a disused underground station—just before war broke out.

When the Second World War ended, in 1945, the treasure was returned to the Museum. The process of examining, cleaning and restoring it began. It was a long, difficult task, but Dr Plenderleith and Mr Herbert Maryon, who were in charge of the work, achieved an almost miraculous success.

Some materials that had been decorated with gold had decayed or vanished, though the gold itself had remained. Some of the silver had perished, the bronze and iron were badly decayed, and leather and wood had shrunk into unrecognizable fragments. But from what looked like a heap of old junk there finally emerged a splendid, glittering collection of jewellery, weapons and personal goods, superbly made and decorated.

The treasure is now on exhibition in the King Edward VII Gallery in the British Museum. The domestic articles include an iron-bound wooden bucket, three bronze cauldrons, a bundle of spears, an iron-hafted battle-axe, and some chainwork. There are also some pieces of a small rectangular harp which had been found in a bronze bowl; the remains of a set of silver-mounted drinking horns, one of them capable of holding six quarts; a great circular silver dish bearing the stamp of the Byzantine Emperor Anastasius, who reigned from A.D. 491–518; a fluted silver bowl which had originally come from somewhere in the Mediterranean area; a silver ladle and a set of six silver bowls (four others were not considered in a fit state to show); and two spoons, ten inches long, one bearing the name 'Saul' in Greek characters, and the other 'Paul'. These may have

139

been presents given when a convert to Christianity was baptized.

Three bronze bowls fitted with loops have given rise to a lot of discussion. Some experts think that they were finger-bowls; others that they were sanctuary lamps.

The dead king's personal equipment contains some amazing objects. One of them is a sword with a jewelled pommel and a golden cross-guard—the blade and the scabbard had rusted together into a solid mass. Another is a circular shield almost three feet across, engraved with birds and dragons. It had been repaired in several places, and was probably a family heirloom. That and an iron helmet had very likely been imported from Sweden, or had been brought to Britain by Aethelhere's father. The helmet was in hundreds of little pieces, and it took one expert six months to fit them together.

Nineteen pieces of gold jewellery which had been made locally can be seen. One of them is a buckle, the finest example of an Anglo-Saxon ornament so far found. It has a pattern of interlaced snakes with a border of animals. There is also a pair of gold shoulder straps, decorated with garnets and blue and white mosaics.

The lid of a purse has a jewelled gold frame decorated with plaques and ivory studs. It has a sliding catch at the bottom shaped like a golden tongue, and is very modern in appearance. The material of the purse itself had rotted away, but the contents remained: thirty-seven golden coins, two which had been rubbed blank, and two small bars of gold. Though the coins were undated it is thought that they were struck in France between the years A.D 650 and 660. This has helped archaeologists to build up a picture of the period and the circumstances surrounding the king's burial.

The symbols of royalty were no less impressive. There was an iron standard with a spiked base, and a heavy whetstone, carved with human masks, which is thought to have been either a sceptre or used for some ceremonial purpose. The standard is more than six feet high and has a ring on

140

top on which proudly stands a stag with spreading antlers. Both these objects, which represent the power of a king and the mystery of royalty, are unique.

It is comforting to think that even experts can be wrong in their preliminary announcements. At the inquest Professor Piggott described the position of the 'body' in the burial chamber, and the first comments in the newspapers showed that archaeologists thought that a body had been buried.

'The body in the ship,' said *The Times* on August 5, 1939, 'is believed to be that of Redwald, King of the East Angles, and it was learned yesterday that he was buried in full armour . . .'

These early mistakes were soon rectified. When it was clear that there was no recognizable evidence of a body, either in the form of ashes or the harder remains like bones and teeth, and when chemical tests had confirmed this, then the true picture stood out. The absence of a body meant that the mighty barrow was built as a monument, not a tomb. It was a memorial to a king whose body was not available when the grave was built.

Whether the king was Aethelhere, as many people think, or whether his brother Anna—a Christian who was actually buried at nearby Blythburgh—had been given this kind of memorial by pagan friends will probably never be known for certain.

Mrs Pretty, who could have sold the treasure for thousands of pounds, died in 1942. The site on which the rest of the barrows still stand has not been opened to the public, though the area has been scheduled as an Ancient Monument. Perhaps some of the mounds may be opened in the future. What will the diggers find? Graves that have already been robbed? Or another hoard of treasure that will make the hearts of archaeologists leap with excitement?

What does the ship-trench look like now? Alas, only a shapeless depression in the ground. During the last war tanks on exercises destroyed the 'ghost ship', which had been covered over with bracken to preserve it as other methods would have been too expensive, and the soil conditions were unfavourable.

Research on the treasures still goes on. Replicas of some of the pieces are on display in the Ipswich Museum. Both professional and amateur archaeologists eagerly await the promised new edition of the British Museum guide, which will give the latest opinions and findings of the experts. The story of Sutton Hoo is still unfinished.

CHAPTER SIXTEEN

THE WELL OF SACRIFICE

WHEN Edward Herbert Thompson, an American Consul in Mexico, gazed down into the sinister darkness of a mysterious well in the ancient city of Chichen Itza, he *knew* that, far down in the murky depths, lay the answers to some of the unsolved mysteries connected with those little-known people of the past, the Mayas. He was also *sure* that the still black waters contained treasure, the gold for which the Spanish conquistadores had lusted so hungrily; and he knew that he would never rest until he had wrested the secrets of the well from the silence and darkness . . .

Thompson had first brought himself to the notice of archaeologists when he was a schoolboy in 1879. A magazine published an article he had written in which he had put forward the idea that the Mayan culture had developed from that of the legendary continent of Atlantis which had been submerged under the Atlantic Ocean. Thompson modified his fanciful ideas as he grew older, but he never lost his fascination with the distant past of Central America. When he joined the American Consular service in Mexico at the age of twenty-five, he was overjoyed to have the opportunity of exploring the jungle ruins.

He arrived in the Yucatan Peninsula, in south-east Mexico, in 1885. He lost no time in setting off on expeditions from Merida, the capital. Accompanied by Indian guides, he visited little-known sites in the jungle, and found others not known at all, hidden by living shrouds of greenery. But of all the fabulous ruins he visited, one in particular held him in thrall by its beauty, its magnificence, and its silent witness to the greatness of its past. The name of the ancient capital was Chichen Itza.

The history of the Mayas is both complicated and vague, and there are large gaps in it. Chichen Itza reached its peak of greatness comparatively late in the story, between the eleventh and thirteenth centuries. The Old Mayan Empire had flourished further south, in Guatemala and Honduras, between the fourth and seventh centuries. There the Mayas built their ceremonial centres and covered their stone monuments with sculptured figures and hieroglyphs which are connected with the calendar—the most accurate calendar the world has ever known.

The Old Empire ended in a way that has produced one of the greatest puzzles of all time. Scholars differ widely as to the date, but some time after the beginning of the seventh century the cities of the south were deserted, one by one. The inhabitants began to move north, and soon the creeping jungle swallowed up all the evidence of their splendid art and architecture.

No one knows why this wholesale emigration happened. There have been many attempts to find an explanation. Did a plague drive the Mayas away from their homes, or was it another kind of epidemic? But there is no evidence that their numbers suddenly thinned. They did not die off, but simply went away. Perhaps there was some kind of upheaval of nature, a flood or a devastating earthquake. But if so, the cities would have tumbled down in ruins; as it is, they are almost perfectly preserved. And there are no signs that the Mayas were conquered by invaders, no hint of the destruction that warfare brings.

One likely explanation of the mysterious move is that, because their methods of agriculture were so primitive, the

Columns at the entrance of the Temple of the Warriors,
Chichen Itza

land became useless, worked out, sterile. The Mayas were forced to find another area of good soil that would grow healthy crops.

But perhaps the most convincing reason proposed is that the people rebelled against the all-powerful priests and leaders as their living conditions steadily grew worse.

The two explanations might well have been combined: failure of crops bringing about a revolt against the priests, whose task it was to ensure a successful harvest. So that when the priests failed to fulfil their promises the over-worked peasants had had enough. They simply deserted the cities which had become symbolic of their miseries and hardships; and the once-despotic priests had to carry on as best they could, which wasn't very well at all.

Then the Mayan culture moved to north-east Yucatan and the neighbouring states of Campeche and Quintana Roo, an area liberally dotted with ancient Mayan sites. It is likely that the waves of migrants settled in the cities already flourishing in Yucatan and the other states over a long period, mingling and inter-marrying with the people living in them, and eventually forming what is known as the New Empire. Chichen Itza—'the wells of the holy Itzas'—was the greatest of the Yucatan cities which absorbed the new-comers from the south.

The sacred well of Chichen Itza was like a vast pit sunk far down into the rock. Trees and thick jungle vegetation grew round its edge. Its walls were scarred with cracks and caves which were the homes of snakes, toads and lizards. Strange tropical shrubs grew out of the fissures. The well was almost two hundred feet in diameter at its widest point, and the surface of the water was sixty feet below the rim.

When Edward Herbert Thompson peered into the well's depths, he shuddered with revulsion at the thought of prob-ing beneath the thick, slimy surface, but knew that it was something that he must do. He could never get out of his mind the legends about the well. One of them in particular haunted him. It was an account written by a Franciscan

146

monk, the Archbishop Diego de Landa. Thompson had read his history of Yucatan, written in 1566, after the manuscript, which had been lost for three hundred years, was discovered in the Royal Library at Madrid in 1863.

Here Heinrich Schliemann comes to mind again. Just as he had believed so fervently in the truth behind the epics of Homer, so Thompson had a similar faith in the observations of de Landa, who had described the great processions from the Temple of Kukulcan—the Feathered Serpent to whom Chichen Itza was consecrated—along the Sacred Way to the sacrificial well.

The priests led, followed by people carrying rich offerings for the gods. Then came a straggling line of human victims, young girls and captive soldiers whose fate was to be hurled into the water to meet certain death in order to persuade the gods to bring an end to drought, pestilence or other disaster. As they approached the well they heard the wailing of pipes and flutes and saw the heaped treasures that would also go over the side at the bidding of the priests . . .

There was another story of the rituals connected with the well, written by a Spanish official named Don Diego Sarmiento de Figueroa in 1579. This too had acted as a spur to Thompson's determination to find the treasure he dreamed of. In addition to describing the processions and ritual sacrifices, de Figueroa added some weird details which both bewildered and intrigued Thompson. After a period of fasting, said de Figueroa, some of the important people of the city visited the well at daybreak and with due ceremony threw the women members of their families into the water, commanding them to beg favours from the gods and to report back what the gods answered!

Apparently nothing happened till high noon. Then the women who had survived the ordeal called out. Ropes were lowered to them, and they were hauled out, almost completely exhausted, as may be imagined. Fires were built round their prostrate bodies and incense burned before them. When the women were sufficiently recovered they

147

told a strange story of men and women who lived beneath the water, either gods or ghosts who answered the questions that were put to them, but who showered blows on the heads of any woman who dared to lift her head to get a better look at them . . .

'I *know* it's a fanciful story,' Thompson told himself, 'but there must be some hard facts behind the myth.'

He had already bought the site on which the ruins of Chichen Itza stood, an old plantation which he hoped to make productive in order to raise money for his excavations. But there was something important he had to do before venturing into the well, and that was to learn how to be a deep-sea diver. He returned to the United States to take instruction. He was soon a proficient diver and was able to use various types of underwater equipment.

Thompson was then in a position to persuade the American Antiquarian Society and Harvard University to finance his scheme. When they agreed, unable to resist his great enthusiasm, he returned to Yucatan, taking with him a dredge and winch, a portable derrick and thirty-foot boom, steel cables, ropes and buckets.

A sounding lead revealed that the water in the well was between seventy-five and eighty feet deep. To discover the most favourable point to begin dredging, Thompson cut logs of wood to the size and weight of an average human and threw them into the water just as the priests had hurled the terrified victims hundreds of years before. Where the logs entered the water was the point chosen for the dredging, on the assumption that the bodies had entered it at that point too.

At last everything was ready. The first dredge sank into the water. The steel cables tautened as the workmen turned the winch-handles to bring it back to the surface.

If Thompson hoped for fabulous treasure at the first attempt, he was sadly disappointed. It was not the gleam of gold or the glitter of precious stones that he saw when the dredge released its contents on to a specially built platform, but dirty brown mud, decayed wood, dead leaves and rotting branches . . . So the dredge was lowered again . . . and again . . . day after day. The pile of refuse grew larger, and the smell got worse.

Thompson began to be gnawed by doubts. *Did* any treasure exist, or had he involved his sponsors in a fruitless task? So far the only bones brought up to the top had been those of animals, including the skeleton of a jaguar; the only artifacts had been a few potsherds. Had the stories of de Landa and de Figueroa been nothing but myths after all?

When the turning-point came it was not spectacular, but it was sufficiently important to revive Thompson's flagging hopes. One day, when the dredge had spewed out its usual unpleasant load, Thompson noticed two yellowish-white round objects that looked strangely out of place among the leaves and mud. His heart began to beat faster as he picked them up and examined them. Surely they had been made by human hands? They had a waxy constituency—could they be balls of resin? He smelled them, then broke off a piece and tasted it. His excitement grew. He put another piece in the hot embers of a fire—and the stench of the mountain of decaying matter gave place to the pungent fragrance of incense!

All Thompson's doubts vanished. He had found some of the sacred incense that had been used in the ancient ceremonies and afterwards thrown into the well as an offering to the gods . . . That night he slept soundly for the first time for weeks.

The balls of resin were the forerunners of many important and exciting finds. Jade figures, ornaments, vases, copper implements and decorated discs followed. There were obsidian knives, axe-heads, tiny bells, and objects of gold, or a copper and gold alloy. And the truth behind the legends was established when the first human skeleton was lifted from the well to join the heap of treasure. It was followed by many others, of men, women and children. De Landa had been right. The well *had* received its living victims, and

Thompson's faith in the sixteenth-century monk's history had been fully justified.

But what about the incredible ritual that de Figueroa had written about? Had that any basis in fact?

One day as Thompson was sitting on the pontoon used for diving operations and gazing into the water, he suddenly realized that it was not as opaque in some places as in others. He had long been fascinated by the way its colour seemed to vary between dark brown, jade green and even blood-red, but its surface was so mirror-like that it was impossible to see beneath it. But on this occasion he could distinctly make out what looked like deeps and hollows under the water.

More astonishing still, he could see the dim outlines of heads and bodies and, most startling of all, he could hear voices—the subdued tones of men talking quietly to each other! This recalled so vividly the ordeal of the Mayan women who had been thrown into the well to talk to the gods that for a moment Thompson wondered whether he had slipped back in time.

Then reason came to his aid, and a few moments of quick thinking gave him the answer to the puzzle and the facts behind the strange belief. The deeps and hollows were the reflections of the caves and cracks in the pitted walls of the well. The human shapes were the reflections of the workmen looking over the well's edge at the water far below. The voices were *their* voices, the sound of which had struck the surface of the water and, by some acoustic trick, then appeared to come from beneath it. So the unfortunate women of old, while struggling and drowning in the well, had mistaken the heads and voices of the priests and nobles high above them for the gods who lived in the inky depths . . .

When the dredge failed to bring up any further objects of value, Thompson decided that the time had come to put into practice his knowledge of diving. It was the only way to recover anything small that the dredge had missed. He had already arranged for a Greek professional diver and his assistant to dive with him. They put on cumbersome canvas suits, round copper helmets, heavy shoes and weighted collars, and prepared to descend.

The native workmen were horrified! Superstitions about the hidden terrors of the well had never completely died out. They were so convinced that Thompson and the Greek divers would never be seen again that each man solemnly shook their hands in formal farewell!

But no ugly monsters or vengeance-seeking god threatened the three divers—only the lizards and snakes which had fallen in from the rocks and shrubs above. There was only one nasty moment when they were in the muddy pit cut by the dredge. Torches were useless and the darkness was almost complete. Suddenly Thompson sensed the presence of a huge object moving slowly towards him, and experienced a moment of panic. It took him quite a time to stop shaking even when he discovered that it was only a tree trunk . . .

The diving operations had very satisfactory results. Many more objects lying at the bottom of the well were found; among them more jade figures, incense balls, dart-throwers, sacrificial knives, fragments of fabric, and skeletons. The sacrificial offerings had all been broken before being thrown into the water. This was because the Mayas believed that everything must be 'killed' before it could be received in the world of spirits.

Then the time came when the sacred well had given up all its treasures and had revealed its secrets. Thompson decided to spend some time in developing his estate, which contained the ruins of Chichen Itza. If his plantation could be made profitable he would be able to afford another exploration into the city's fascinating past. Unfortunately his plan failed. 1910 was a year of revolutions and insurrections, and Thompson found himself the target of revolutionary violence. His hacienda was ransacked and destroyed, and many of his records and relics were burned and broken.

This misfortune was the prelude to an even greater disaster. The actual monetary value of the finds from the sacred well was comparatively small; the true value lay in the light they would shed on the culture and religion of the unknown Mayas. But rumour got busy, and finally everybody 'knew' that the treasures were worth at least a half a million dollars! The Mexican Government accepted the rumour as truth and demanded possession of the gold. But the treasure had been sent to Harvard University, and the authorities there would not give it up. In revenge the Mexicans seized Thompson's estate and held it to ransom, demanding half a million pesos before they would return it.

They might just as well have asked for ten million! Thompson fought to get back his home for year after weary year, but he never did regain possession of Chichen Itza and its sacred well. He died in 1935, old and tired, but still struggling.

Thompson, a man with a passion, had at least the satisfaction of achieving much of what he had set his heart on doing. He contributed greatly to the scanty store of knowledge of the Mayas, and he silenced the scoffers who said there was no truth behind the old legends. Thanks to him the people of Chichen Itza are no longer shadows.

CHAPTER SEVENTEEN

BACKGROUND AND BEGINNINGS

ABOUT the year 550 B.C. Nabonidus, the last king of Babylon (who was more interested in collecting antiques than in ruling), investigated the ruins of a temple dedicated to the god Shamash and discovered, thirty feet below the ground, a foundation-stone which, he claimed, had been laid by King Naram-sin three thousand years before.

This date was very much of a guess, and has since been reduced by more than a thousand years, but Nabonidus's error does not detract from his achievement. He was, in fact, so much more interested in the past than in his own present that he left the defence of the kingdom to his son. When Cyrus II of Persia invaded Babylon in 538 B.C. Nabonidus yielded without a struggle. He died soon afterwards, possibly of frustration because he could no longer add to his collection of statues!

In A.D. 1954, Mr W. F. Grimes, at that time the Director of the London Museum, digging on a building site among the ruins of bomb-pitted London, discovered the marble head of a Roman god, hidden for perhaps seventeen hundred years, in the remains of a temple dedicated to Mithras, whose religion was at one time the rival of Christianity.

From Nabonidus to Mr Grimes, from a ruined temple in Babylon to one in London, more than 2,500 years have passed. Yet there has hardly been a time when men have not been digging, exploring, searching—in temples and tombs, caves and quarries, graves and galleries, hills and hollows; under the ground and in the sea. What have they been looking for? Why do they do it? What is this passion that consumes them so that they *must* dig into the past and feel, when they turn up a fragment of pot or a hand-chipped stone, such satisfaction, such a sense of triumph?

We can only reconstruct the life of people who lived before there were written records by finding and examining the material things they left behind them—weapons and tools, the contents of their rubbish dumps, the remains of their graves, houses, palaces and temples. And that is what the science of archaeology is about: the study of men's relics and the attempt to relate them to their lives.

Can archaeology be a science, though, when chance plays such a large part in its processes, when reasoning has to be partnered by guesswork and leaps of the imagination much oftener than with a pure science?

The scientific method certainly enters archaeology. Every year more and more use is being made of techniques that science has developed. But archaeology is also closely allied to history, which is not a natural science, as well as to geology, the science of the earth's crust. The archaeologist needs the help of surveyor, geologist, engineer, laboratory technician, chemist and physicist. Does this make him just a grubber after dusty facts? No, because he must also seek the help of artist, architect, photographer and historian. What does that make him, then?

Let us shrug our shoulders and get out of the difficulty by calling archaeology a science, but an inexact one; and an archaeologist a scientist with the extra qualities of an artist. Whatever he is, his first job is to *dig up people*; that is, to relate the *things* he uncovers to the *people* who made and used them. Secondly, he has to *write history* by putting his finds in an orderly time sequence, rather like popping pieces of jigsaw puzzle into their right places on the board.

In order to avoid confusion we must next make a distinction between the prehistorian and the archaeologist. The former deals only with the time before written or visual records existed, when only material remains are left to be interpreted.

The shape, texture and decoration of a pot found in a grave with a skeleton will tell us roughly when the man lived and something of his culture, but it won't tell us the whole story—who the man was, or how many children he had. An arrow-head embedded in a spinal vertebra, such as was found at Maiden Castle, will provide the information that puts the man in his period and tells us that he died in battle and who he was fighting; but we shall never know what the victim's thoughts were as he fell dying, or how his family mourned him. Prehistory, then, is full of gaps and guesses. The plot of the story of early man is often clear in outline, but it lacks human details.

The archaeologist is, of course, a prehistorian, but he also extends his activities to later times, when inscriptions on palace and temple walls, on clay tablets and papyrus rolls, provide a check to guesswork, and offer more detailed and accurate information. Indeed, the scope of archaeology stretches right up to yesterday.

That empty baked-beans tin you put in the dustbin after supper is now part of history. It tells a little story. We know, at least, whether you prefer baked beans with or without tomato sauce! Archaeologists have recently begun to take an interest in such comparatively late-in-time subjects as the medieval villages which were deserted after the Black Death, or when arable land was taken over for sheep enclosures between 1450 and 1550; and in the canals, mills, railways, tramroads and bridges brought by the Industrial Revolution in the eighteenth and nineteenth centuries. This is a far cry from the bones of Neanderthal Man, who lived a hundred thousand years ago, but it is just as much a part of archaeology.

What have archaeologists, from Nabonidus to Professor Grimes and other distinguished men and women of today, done for history? What have they told us of man's story? While we must remember that we know only a part of what there is to know, and that what is unknown is like the submerged part of an iceberg, the achievements of archaeologists have been tremendous, and we have a pretty good idea what our ancestors were up to.

This story has been reconstructed by the men who have found the clues and have tried to interpret their meaning. They have not been content to say, 'Here is a pot made by a Bronze Age woman', or 'Here is a bison painted on a cave wall', but have asked themselves, 'What did the woman put in the pot and how did she get the food?' and 'Why did primitive man paint on the inaccessible walls of caves, and what did he paint with?'

By such questions, multiplied a thousandfold, we have been given our picture of how our ancestors lived, what they ate, how they built and who they fought; what they were skilled at, what they traded in, and where they went. What is still unsure is: what were they thinking? What did they believe in? What were their plans, their hopes and fears?

Archaeologists are at a disadvantage, of course, in getting to the scene hundreds, thousands, or hundreds of thousands of years after things have happened, when evidence has crumbled, decayed or perished. Wood and leather shrink or turn to dust. Some metals corrode. Things made of stone, pottery, glass and gold, and bones are what the archaeologist has to try to make sense of, and he must not be in a hurry about it. Sometimes his conclusions are wrong and the picture gets distorted. Further discoveries, further study, and comparison with similar evidence found elsewhere usually put things right.

Archaeology is really a very new science as far as technique is concerned. Though we have called Nabonidus the first archaeologist, he did not have the help of the prismatic compass or radio-active carbon! Until a few hundred years ago not many people were interested in the relics of past ages that turned up under the spade or plough, or deformed the face of the countryside like large carbuncles or stone teeth. The grass-covered burial mounds we call *barrows* were thought to be giants' graves. The lines and circles of standing stones which once formed part of a construction used for religious or magical purposes were explained by stories of girls who were turned to stone for dancing on a Sunday, or of the devil hurling stones about in a fit of temper.

It is true that all through history there have been men who collected antiquities, but their interest was in the beauty and value of the objects themselves rather than in the light they might throw on the life of past ages.

The first man in England to contribute towards real archaeological study was John Leland, whom Henry VIII appointed as 'King's Antiquary', the first and last man to have that title. In the 1530's and 1540's Leland travelled about the country searching for records of ancient history in the libraries of colleges and monasteries. He also made notes about the old monuments and medieval buildings he came across, and some of the prehistoric remains. He intended to write a great history of ancient things in England, but the task was too much for him as his health broke down.

William Camden, born in 1551, was another antiquarian who made similar journeys up and down the country. When he was thirty-five he published his most famous work, the *Britannia*, which was revised and enlarged right up to 1806, and which led to great public interest in the relics of the past which were all around if people only bothered to look for them. The real value of Camden's work was the way he demolished many of the historical myths that had made Geoffrey of Monmouth's *British History,* written in the twelfth century, so unreliable.

During the reign of Charles II, John Aubrey, encouraged by the king, made some careful records of prehistoric monuments in Surrey and Wiltshire, and aroused interest in the Bronze Age sanctuary of Avebury. Unfortunately, his theory that Avebury and Stonehenge were Druidic temples was responsible for a misconception that has lasted for hundreds of years; right up to the present day, in fact. Though Aubrey's theory has been completely exploded, the Druids of today, mild and harmless versions of the barbaric Celtic priests who are supposed to have practised human sacrifice, still amble round Stonehenge on Midsummer Eve and provide a comic spectacle for sightseers and cameramen.

The first practical archaeologists appeared in the eighteenth century. The Society of Antiquaries was formed in 1717. Collecting was still an obsession, but there was a more serious side to the work of the Society. Its first secretary was William Stukeley, a notable archaeologist, whose charming drawings and careful plans of Stonehenge and Avebury have been very useful to later students. He also excavated some of the nearby barrows in a more scientific way than anyone else had done.

Stukeley's early field work was a model of accurate observation and careful analysis, but he later plunged into romantic and far-fetched theories that made nonsense of his work. He became an arch-Druidist, and declared that the priests of Stonehenge were Phoenicians who had come to Britain soon after Noah's Flood and founded a religion that had later developed into the Church of England!

Fortunately, the end of the eighteenth century brought a new approach to archaeology, and many fanciful ideas were put in their place by the publications of the Society of Antiquaries.

The excavation of barrows became a popular pastime for country ladies and gentlemen. They did not do the actual digging, of course. Labourers were hired for the hard work, while the gentry played games or picnicked on the grass. Methods of excavation were crude. A hole was dug down the middle of the burial mound, and if there was anything at the bottom it was hauled up and taken away. No plans were drawn, no written records of any kind were made, and as a result an incalculable number of vital clues were lost to future archaeologists.

Then came Sir Richard Colt Hoare. He lived in Wiltshire, a county rich in prehistoric remains, and excavated 379 barrows in the course of his antiquarian career. But he worked carefully, making exact records. His aim was admirable.

'We speak from facts, not theory,' he wrote. 'I shall not seek among the fanciful regions of Romance an origin for our Wiltshire barrows.'

He had to admit, after ten years' work, that he was still ignorant of the 'authors of these sepulchral memorials', and he despaired that the history of the stupendous temples at Avebury and Stonehenge would ever emerge from the thick fog that seemed to surround all prehistoric things.

But the fog of prehistory did begin to lift, and light began to shine through in Denmark. Christian Jorgensen Thomsen, the curator of the National Museum at Copenhagen, was the man responsible. He was the first man to put forward the idea of the 'Three Age System'. Men, he said, had first lived in an age of stone, then had learned the use of metals; bronze first, and later iron; and he arranged all the prehistoric objects in his museum in that order.

That seems an obvious enough idea to us now, but it was revolutionary in 1836 and, like all new ideas, provoked much opposition. Thomsen based his theory on the stone or metal tools that were found together on a site, and the types which were found in layers either above or below other types. Stratification, as it is called, is now the basis of all archaeological methods.

1859 was an explosive year for archaeologists. For some time previously a ferment of ideas had been coming to the boil—such as those of Thomsen and other European antiquarians and geologists. There were Father MacEnery's and William Pengelly's discoveries of flint implements in the same layer as the bones of Ice Age animals under a stalagmite floor in Kent's Cavern in south Devon. There was the confirmation of Boucher de Perthes's finds at Abbeville. Then, in 1859, came Charles Darwin's book, *The Origin of Species*, in which he set out his reasons for the long antiquity of man, and man's gradual evolution from ape-like ancestors. The resulting fireworks were noisy indeed . . .

Darwin was attacked fiercely, and no less fiercely defended, and in the end his ideas prevailed. Gone for ever was the date 4004 B.C. for the creation of the world, calculated by Archbishop Ussher a century before; and 'October 23, 4004 B.C., at nine o'clock in the morning,' Dr John Lightfoot's extension of the fantasy, disappeared in a snort of laughter.

The age of archaeological science had begun, and pioneers like Auguste Mariette and Gaston Maspero, Sir Wallis Budge, Sir Flinders Petrie, Bernard Grenfell, Sir Austen Henry Layard, Sir Henry Rawlinson, George Smith and Heinrich Schliemann blazed a trail that opened up the world of the past to the twentieth century, when new scientific methods came to the archaeologist's aid.

An archaeologist is a man who is tormented with curiosity and is determined not to rest until he has satisfied it. He is an adventurer and explorer, whether he journeys half across the world or strolls into the field next to his house. He must be physically strong, able to endure heat and cold and the hazards of desert, jungle and mountain.

He is often argumentative and obstinate, sometimes secretive, always short of money. (There are many people in positions of power who pretend an interest in activities like archaeology, but most of them turn a beady and unresponsive eye on applications for help.) He is a patient man, and time means nothing to him. He knows that years of toil might produce no more than will fill a shoe-box while amateurs and children are accidentally stumbling across gaudy treasures that will make sensational headlines in the newspapers; but that does not worry him at all. Sometimes he writes articles and books, gives lectures and becomes famous on television; but often nobody knows of him or his work but fellow workers in the same field. He digs and scratches like a mole, climbs like a monkey or dives like a seal. He is indeed a curious animal.

CHAPTER EIGHTEEN

GET DIGGING!

THE stories of important and exciting discoveries told in this book are only a small part of the whole story of archaeology. Much more can be found in the list of books at the end. But the story is still unfinished.

Archaeology is going on somewhere in the world all the time. Men, women and young people are digging, sifting, planning, drawing. They are getting muddy, dirty and tired, with aching muscles and aching heads. They are finding their tasks exciting—or boring. Their patience is inexhaustible, and their physical condition as tough as if they were in an Olympic team.

They wonder sometimes why they bother to carry on, but their doubts disappear immediately something turns up, even if it is only a fragment of pottery or a piece of rusty iron, a coin, a single tooth or a strangely marked stone. They know they are helping to unearth the past of the human race and adding a minute fraction to our knowledge of the way people lived, how they built, what they worshipped, where they travelled, with whom they traded, and how they spent their leisure.

The lure of archaeology is in its mystery, the exploration of the unknown, the strange feeling of turning a corner and not knowing what you are going to find. The much publicized accidental discoveries, such as the Lascaux Cave, act as a spur to many diggers. Who knows what is going to turn up under the next spadeful? What new civilization, or new assessment of an old one, will the season's work reveal?

Excavators at work

What thrill there is in being the first person for thousands of years to touch the tarnished gold of a woman's ornament or turn over in the fingers a heap of blackened coins that were last handled by a Roman merchant . . . In such cases time seems to disappear, and yesterday and today merge.

Archaeology shows us that loving, hating, fighting, killing, making beautiful things, worshipping the unknown, seeking shelter, bringing up children, have been going on for a long, long time; that people have not changed, even though their habits and customs may have. The Neanderthal woman, cradling a dead child killed by a cave-bear, is no different from the woman of Hiroshima who, in 1945, clasped the charred body of her atom-blasted baby and gazed in bewilderment at the smoky sky. The desperate defenders of Maiden Castle might be the same soldiers who, in the last war, fought against hopeless odds at Singapore. The pomp and circumstance of an Egyptian pharaoh's burial is echoed in the solemn rites which now attend the death of a king. There is so much of the present bound up in the past, and so much of the past comes alive again in our own times. That is why archaeology never loses its fascination, why there will always be this quest for our ancestors.

Many young people, reading about the great discoveries, become fired with enthusiasm to join an excavation, but often they don't know how to go about it. There are several ways in which one can get practical experience in digging. No one need be put off by the feeling that it is only professional archaeologists who have all the fun. As a matter of fact, archaeology depends largely on people for whom it is a hobby or a part-time occupation. The people who earn a living at it are a small minority.

If you *must* be a professional archaeologist, however, you can do it by joining the Civil Service, the staff of a University where archaeology is taught, or a museum. The Civil Service offers archaeological appointments in the Ancient Monuments Inspectorate of the Ministry of Works, the Royal Commission on Historical Monuments, and the Archaeology Section of the Ordnance Survey. A university degree is a basic requirement. The function of these departments is to maintain the structure of historic buildings, to preserve monuments such as hill-forts or barrows, to make full records of them, county by county, and to prepare archae-

163

ological maps. The actual excavation of sites is occasionally carried out.

There are further opportunities for professionals as museum curators and assistants, technicians, draughtsmen and photographers, and they are concerned with the preservation of archaeological finds. There are many kinds of museums, some large ones with separate departments of archaeology which cover many parts of the world, and smaller ones which deal only with local finds. The excavation of local sites is occasionally arranged by a neighbourhood museum, but there are no full-time jobs going on any excavations. Digs are seasonal events, dependent on the weather. When a dig is finished the assistants are paid off; though in the Near East, where excavations are long-term affairs, a 'temporary' post may last for some years.

Unless your interest is so great that it will take you through to a university degree (taking in on the way courses in ancient history, probably Latin, Greek, geography, economics and modern languages), then it is best to decide that you will remain an amateur! If so, you will still be able to do very worth-while work. Whatever you happen to be—doctor, teacher, milkman, miner or housewife—you can spend your holidays and week-ends in getting training and experience.

Look out for the notices of lectures organized by universities or local archaeological societies. Join such a society, meet other people with the same passion and get the chance of helping on excavations. Reading, too, is very important. There are many books which cover all aspects of the subject. There are also periodicals published by societies for their members which contain the latest news of what is happening in the archaeological world.

Consult your museum freely and frequently, and visit others when you are on holiday. There are more than nine hundred museums in Great Britain, and they will give you many hours of happy browsing in the archaeology sections. Try to *feel* the exhibits as well as see them. Then you will know what it is to be a caveman handling a flint tool. If everything is locked away under glass, of course, then you will have to make a personal friend of the curator!

Above all, volunteer for practical work on a dig. Even untrained people are welcome, and you will soon get the experience to make you a valuable part of the outfit. Every summer, hundreds of amateur archaeologists pick up their trowels and make tracks for a dig. Your companions may be students, housewives, nurses, typists, doctors and scientists. Very often camp is set up on the site, with running water and lavatories provided by the Ministry of Works. Meals are cooked by volunteers, and a sing-song round the camp fire at night adds to the pleasure. You may also find enthusiasts from overseas, for in some foreign countries amateurs are not allowed to dig.

The digging season lasts from Easter to October, and in Britain alone scores of excavations are started. Most of them are supervised by Ministry of Works experts; others are organized by museums, universities, and archaeological societies. The digs are extremely varied and cover all periods, from the earliest prehistoric to the eighteenth century. Iron Age and Roman sites are perhaps the most common.

During 1964 a medieval moat was explored near Birmingham, some Roman defences at Ancaster in Lincolnshire, and a Roman village at Winterton in the same county. In Somerset caves were investigated, a medieval castle in Montgomeryshire, some pre-Roman earthworks at Stanwyck in Yorkshire, and a Saxon town at Thetford in Norfolk, the latter threatened with obliteration by the building of a new housing estate.

In fact, there is such a lot of work going on every year, such a great demand for volunteer diggers, and so many volunteers offering their services, that the Council for British Archaeology (8, St Andrew's Place, Regent's Park, London, N.W.1), which co-ordinates the efforts of 255 local archaeological societies, 19 universities and 81 museums, produces a monthly calendar from March to September. It costs 7s 6d a year, and it lists the sites where people are needed, the kind of work that has to be done—heavy digging, surveying, cooking, photography, etc—whether beginners can attend or experienced diggers only; and there is also a list of week-end courses and summer schools.

Every year the Council receives 2,500 enquiries from home and abroad. Every year hundreds of people, both young and old, find themselves either on a bare moorland, in the depths of a wood, on the outskirts of a village, on a demolition site in a town, or on wasteland by a river or factory. There, in cramped working conditions, perhaps knee-deep in mud, drenched with rain or scorched by sun, they will work for long hours with little or no pay. And at the end they will declare that they have had the best holiday of their lives!

What do you actually do on a dig? Well, it is not all heavy digging! In fact, the director of a dig prefers to use professional workmen if he can afford them. The volunteer is engaged mainly on excavating the different archaeological levels that are arrived at during the digging, and this calls for very careful work with small tools. Sometimes, when finds are made, especially on sites connected with Iron Age and Roman times, you will have to wash potsherds and bones, mark them and pack them away. At other times you will find yourself attached to the handles of a wheelbarrow for what seems a lifetime . . .

You will wear old clothes, naturally, strong shoes or wellingtons, a macintosh and leather gloves. You will not be expected to provide your own tools, though many people prefer to take their own trowel and guard it as jealously as a tennis-player his racket. The more digs you volunteer for, and the more experience you get, the more responsibility you will be given. It will be a proud moment when you can talk to a 'real' archaeologist on *his* level.

The amateur archaeologist will not limit his interest to holidays and week-ends. He will be looking round him all the time, when he is cycling, walking, or travelling by car, train or plane; and he will as often as possible carry with him a map of the area he is exploring.

Gravel beds on the sides of valleys and in valley bottoms; limestone caves and rock shelters; the top layers of earth above quarries or chalk-pits; the holes made by demolition workers before houses and factories are built or new roads laid down; these are the sort of places that yield evidence of past occupation. Bits of broken pottery, bones, flint and stone implements, flakes of flint, coins and lumps of corroded metals; these are the more obvious objects that might turn up.

Never neglect a newly ploughed field. Depressions in the ground, trenches and ancient rubbish-pits might mean an occupation site; a filled-up well could have belonged to a medieval village that has disappeared. On high ground mounds and barrows stand out like huge warts, and large stones in lines or circles mark the spot where Bronze Age people built their mysterious temples. Both town and countryside are *full* of possibilities . . .

When you have found something that intrigues you, don't start to dig straight away, and don't carry your finds away from the site. Instead, mark the spot, then tell your teacher, as the boys who found the Lascaux Cave did, or inform the curator of your local museum. If the site turns out to be worth investigating, then the excavation will have to become official after negotiations have taken place with the owner of the land; and, though you will doubtless be taken on as an assistant, your own enthusiastic probing will have to give way to the scientific methods of the professional.

You will find that the newspapers are a good source of information about archaeological discoveries. *The Times* and the *Guardian*, for instance, report regularly even minor finds. Your local paper will be sure to run a story about anything that is found in the neighbourhood. When you hear or read of something in that line, hurry off at once to the site, tell the director of your interest in archaeology and politely ask permission to hang around and do any jobs that might be needed. Listen to what the experts are saying, and you will pick up a lot of valuable information. The day will no doubt come when you will be entrusted with the more finicky tasks, and you will exchange your wheelbarrow for a paint-brush!

When you have had a lot of experience of archaeology in the field; when you have read a great deal and have learned some of the inner secrets of the subject; if your enthusiasm is as great as when you first started; and if the idea of doing any other kind of job for the rest of your life appals you, then the time has come to decide that you will be a professional and leave your amateur days behind. Then you will have to start working for that university degree . . .

In the great majority of cases young people who have been caught by the digging fever have, through force of circumstances, to content themselves with archaeology as a hobby, a fascinating spare time occupation that provides compensation for the drudgery of the daily job. But whatever may happen in the future, the thing to do now is—get digging!

CHAPTER NINETEEN

FINDING A SITE

IN the old days of archaeology, before the time of General Pitt-Rivers and Sir Flinders Petrie, standards of excavating were low, as we have seen. Tombs were ruthlessly robbed of their antiquities to satisfy the greed of collectors, and methods of excavation were so inefficient that as much valuable evidence was lost as was gained. Countless finds were disregarded, broken or just thrown away.

Things are very different nowadays. The object of digging is not simply to discover treasure, but to find out what went on at each level of the site, in order to understand the life of the people who, at different times, lived there. Evidence can so easily be destroyed if it is not properly observed and recorded.

The term 'stratification' has already been mentioned. The layers of earth which interest the archaeologist are those which have been laid down during, or since, the time men have occupied a particular place, or where the soil has been disturbed by such things as trenches or banks. The principle of stratification is that an object left on or in the soil at a certain time will be found at a lower level than one left at a later date. Thus an excavator begins by uncovering the top layers of a site which contain the latest objects, and works downwards to the earliest deposits. Then he can

169

build up a picture of what happened—how one building succeeded another, how one was perhaps destroyed by fire, earthquake or enemy action; how tools, weapons and ornaments developed, and how the lives of the people who lived there changed too.

Of course, before an archaeologist can start digging, he must have a site to dig. There is not much point in shifting tons of soil if he is not sure that there is going to be anything to find. Experts don't just go to any old field, hill or quarry, stick a spade in the ground and spit on a lucky sixpence!

There are many ways in which evidence of underground archaeological interest may be found. One of them is when ground containing prehistoric relics has been disturbed, either by natural means such as wind and water or the burrowing of animals, or by the activities of men—ploughing, ditching, quarrying or building.

In sandy places ancient structures are sometimes uncovered when the sand has been blown away by the wind. The famous Stone Age village of Skara Brae in the Orkneys, with its stone walls and furniture, was exposed in this way. The action of water can be seen when coastlines are being eaten away by waves and the relics of people who lived near the coast are washed out of the cliffs.

The eroding of river banks has often led to the discovery of material, for people have always liked to live by rivers. Drought, too, has been responsible for finds. When rivers and lakes dry up, or the level of the water falls considerably (as happened at Obermeilen in 1854), the deposits of silt and decayed vegetable matter have yielded wooden articles or woven fabrics that in other conditions would have disintegrated completely. Peat-cutters in Ireland, North Wales and the Fen district turn up such things—though there has not yet been a British Tollund Man!

Coins, potsherds and flint tools are occasionally found in the holes made by rabbits, foxes and badgers, brought nearer the surface by scrabbling feet.

When we come to man's activities, the opportunities for finding evidence of prehistoric man seem endless. Ploughing frequently turns up a site which was only a few feet from the surface; and coins, pottery, ornaments and the debris of old buildings have come to light. When ditches or holes for fences are being dug, traces of the past may be revealed. This happened at Lullingstone in Kent and brought to light a Roman villa. Chalk quarries may produce anything from an axe-head to a human skull.

One of the few happy by-products of the last war was the clearing of sites for rebuilding after the devastation of the Blitz, and the consequent unearthing of innumerable objects of archaeological significance. With the growth of housing estates and new towns, and high blocks of flats and offices which require very deep foundations, the soil of centuries has to be cleared away, and the treasures thus exposed help to fill our museums. It is a pity that mechanical excavators scoop up such great quantities of earth at a time so that many small objects disappear unnoticed into the trucks, but some builders are sufficiently concerned to keep a look-out for things of possible value to the archaeologist.

There are, of course, many antiquities which, by their size, cannot fail to make their presence known; and we do not need the help of wind or water to see earthworks like Maiden Castle or Silbury Hill, the West Kennet long barrow, or huge monuments like Stonehenge and Avebury. In the past some of these have been attacked by enthusiastic but unskilled amateurs, and some have been looted for 'treasure', but many have survived for the excavator to tackle with modern techniques.

When there have been neither natural nor human agencies to point to a possible site for excavation, and when an observer on the ground has failed to see anything out of the ordinary, then we bring the aeroplane and helicopter into service. Air photographs reveal the 'ghosts' of buried buildings by showing inequalities in the ground which are invisible to anyone at ground level, and by shadow, soil and crop marks.

When the sun is low, shadows are often cast by mounds and banks which may have been worn down almost to ground level. Photographs taken from the air when these shadows are longest have shown ancient field-boundaries and lynchets (soil which has collected in banks at the bottom of a cultivated field on a slope). Frost or snow lodging in hollow ground may also show low banks. Shallow flooding can bring out differences in ground levels not otherwise noticeable.

Crop marks are the variations in height or colour of a growing crop. As the strength of a crop depends largely on the amount of moisture and nourishment it gets from the soil, it grows higher and greener when the subsoil holds moisture in its lower levels. Where trenches or pits have once been dug and then filled in, the earth is looser and more porous than the earth surrounding them, and plants can put out longer roots and grow taller and healthier. On the other hand, a crop growing over buried Roman roads, for instance, or over the remains of buildings, will be more stunted because the soil is shallower and holds less water.

At certain stages of a crop's growth, and especially during dry weather when the ground lacks moisture, the variations can be seen on photographs. The direction of walls or the plans of buildings can be drawn with reasonable accuracy before the first spade is thrust into the ground.

Differences in the colour of soil become apparent when fields have been ploughed and nothing is growing. Barrows and earthworks which have been razed to ground level show up on photographs as light marks on darker ground. What were once walls of chalk or rubble appear as light strips. Buried ditches show up dark. These differences are due to the amount of humus, which is darkest when wet, in the subsoil.

Of course air photographs also reveal markings which have nothing to do with ancient things, although they are

An aerial photograph shows features not noticeable at ground level

sometimes mistaken for them—the plough-lines across a
field; levelled-off ditches; light soil which ploughing has
brought to the surface; sheep and cows which look from
a height like white, brown or black dots; the places where
haystacks, manure heaps or trees have been. The archaeologist has to bring all his skill to the interpretation of a

photograph before he can decide if there is anything of interest that needs to be investigated.

On one occasion aerial photographs suggested an important henge site near Weybridge in Surrey. Another Stonehenge! thought the experts, and hurried to the spot. Alas, what they found was a large circle of concrete blocks which had been the mooring platform for barrage balloons during the last war! But air photography has also been responsible for the discovery of Iron Age hill-forts, Woodhenge and the Stonehenge Avenue, and the 'Big Rings' at Dorchester in Oxfordshire.

Another kind of photography has been successfully used in Italy, where there are hundreds of stone tombs built by a mysterious people called the Etruscans. To find out whether a tomb is worth excavating, Italian archaeologists use a pole which has a tiny camera and flash apparatus at one end. This is pushed through a hole made in the tomb wall and into the burial chamber itself, and a photograph of the interior is taken by a control on the end of the pole which remains above ground. 450 tombs have been investigated in four months by using this flash-synchronized micro-camera, echo-sounding apparatus and periscope.

One method often used to search out a possible site is bosing, which means simply thumping the ground with a heavy hammer or a saucer-shaped weight on the end of a pole. If the weight does not accidentally land on your toes you will hear a dull thud, but the sound varies according to what kind of soil is just below the surface. Ground which has never been disturbed gives a much deader, less sonorous, sound than ground which is over an ancient ditch or pit. Chalky countryside with a sparse top soil is favourable for bosing, which was practised by Sir Richard Colt Hoare in the early nineteenth century, and also by General Pitt-Rivers.

Another method is to probe with a strong pointed steel rod with a T-shaped handle at regular intervals over a given area. Some soils are much easier to penetrate than others;

those, for instance, which cover a ditch. If there are hidden building foundations the probe will not sink so far into the ground. The various soundings are recorded on a graph, and the nature of what is under the ground can be surmised.

A more modern way of probing is by the electrical resistivity method, using a megger. This is a very sensitive transistorized instrument which measures the resistance of an electric current. Electrodes in the form of steel rods are inserted into the ground at measured intervals, and current from a hand-generator is passed between them. The electrical pressure which is recorded varies according to the amount of water in the soil. The more saturated the soil, the smaller will be the drop in voltage. The steel rods are moved from place to place, and the readings on the megger are, as in the simpler method, recorded in graph form. A high resistance gives a peak on the graph and indicates something like a hidden wall. A trough on the graph suggests the presence of a prehistoric ditch.

Resistivity surveying is a laborious process, and natural features are recorded as well as man-made ones. But it gives satisfactory results, and saves time when it is a question of either using an instrument or digging up a large expanse of ground with pick and shovel when the actual position of antiquities is uncertain.

The proton magnetometer, a device which is being developed by Dr M. J. Aitken of the Oxford University Archaeological Research Laboratory, is a new aid to the field archaeologist, and is already producing valuable results. It is based on the principle that the humus in soil which has in the past been disturbed, as when a pit has been dug or a ditch excavated, is more magnetic than subsoil—though at the moment no one is sure why this should be so. The magnetometer, which consists of a 'detector bottle' suspended under a wooden tripod connected by a cable with an indicating meter, records the greater magnetic strength of humus-rich soils, and thus helps to locate man-made structures which have caused soil disturbances.

175

The apparatus can also show the presence of buried iron, but of course cannot tell the difference between a buried water pipe of A.D. 1968 and an iron knife of 968 B.C.! Such things as pottery kilns, burnt houses, iron swords, and filled-in ditches and pits have been found.

During the last war, mine detectors were used to indicate that metal landmines were hidden in the ground. As you know, to step on an explosive landmine means that you will be exploded too! When plastic landmines were used instead the usefulness of the mine detector was reduced; but in peacetime it has found another function by detecting metallic objects which are buried just below the surface of the ground. The instrument will not give results if they are more than a few inches below. Brooches, rings, coins and knives are among the things which have been found.

CHAPTER TWENTY

HOW OLD?

ONE of the often incomprehensible things about archaeology is the way the approximate age of an object taken from its earthy or rocky hiding-place is arrived at. Why should it, as an expert may confidently state, be 20,000 years old? Why not 30,000, 40,000—or 400? How do they do it? Is it guesswork or a confidence trick?

Well, it used to be guesswork, and some of the guesses have turned out to be surprisingly correct; but nowadays science, both in the field and in the laboratory, has taken over. The various methods, or combination of methods, which are available enable us to establish the time at which something was made, thrown away, or died, with such accuracy that a time-chart of the past can be constructed that most people will accept.

The first way of dating a find is by stratification. The position of the find is compared with its surroundings to determine in what layer of earth in a sequence of layers the object lay. In the simplest terms, the older the layer the older the object. Unfortunately, things are not always as simple as that. During the earth's long history things have happened to disturb its symmetry. Volcanic action, pressure which causes older rocks to creep gradually over younger ones, floods, earthquakes—these have all in their time caused the earth's crust to shrink, crack, bend and stretch like a crazy contortionist, so that the tidy composition of rock layers has got very muddled, and precise dating by the principle of stratification cannot always be made accurately.

When human remains are found they can usually be related to one of the periods of the Great Ice Age, either when the ice-caps had retreated and given way to warmer climatic conditions, or when they were advancing, bringing colder weather. When animal remains are found with those of humans the species of animal indicates whether it (and therefore the man) was living during a warm or a cold spell. The mammoth and the woolly rhinoceros, for instance, lived in colder conditions, while the crocodile and hippopotamus flourished in an inter-glacial period.

Then, too, the type of vegetation differed greatly at different times in the past. Some trees and plants liked cold and damp conditions, others preferred them warm and dry. The pollen shed from flowers, which has remained in the soil and has resisted decay, can be examined and put in its period; for the pollen of each plant differs in size and shape from every other. Pollen analysis, as this method of dating is called, has enabled us to build up a pattern of vegetation since the last glaciation.

Our knowledge of the dates of Mesolithic and early Neolithic men come from this kind of evidence, though it has to be checked by a more direct method, such as radioactive carbon dating, which will be described later. In later Neolithic times much more accurate evidence comes from the history of the first civilizations of the Near East, when men found it necessary to make records of their work and the reigns of their kings. From about 3,000 B.C. we can be sure that our dates for historical events are reasonably accurate.

This does not apply to most of Europe, however, and certainly not to Britain. Until it was conquered by the Romans in A.D. 43 there is nothing in the way of written history. We have to relate events in the Mediterranean countries and the Near East to any influence they may have had on western Europe, or to find objects that had their origin in the east and had been taken by traders to the west, to be able to make precise datings. For example, a particular kind of bead made in Egypt about 1,400 B.C. has been found in Middle Bronze Age burial sites in Britain, and so we can arrive at a date for the latter.

The dating of trees is made by dendrochronology, a rather off-putting word which simply means using the ring growth of tree remains to find out when they were living, and relating the result to objects found with the remains of the trees.

Most trees add a ring of growth in their trunk every year. If we can count the rings from the outside near the bark inwards to the centre, we know the age of the tree. This sounds easy, but it can be complicated by the formation of extra rings, or by indistinct divisions between them.

Tree-ring dating requires specimens to cross-date; that is, finding in different trees the same ring patterns, each series of rings representing the same period of years. Then the outer ring pattern of a tree cut down years ago can be matched with the inner ring pattern of a tree that was cut down yesterday; and so, by taking trees of overlapping age and working backwards, a scale of dates can be built up.

There are large areas of the world where dendrochronology cannot be used, but the American south-west, northern Mexico, parts of the Arctic regions, Turkey, Egypt, and various places in Europe are favourable.

Fluorine dating is an aid which gives very useful results in checking the age-relation between bones and the deposit in which they have been found. Fortunately for the archaeologist, bones absorb fluorine at a constant rate. The longer a bone has been buried, the more fluorine it contains. Thus, if the bones of a cave-bear occur accidentally in the same layer as a Bronze Age skeleton, the animal remains will contain more fluorine than the man's. The ages of the two sets of bones can be calculated quite accurately, and the man's period can be further checked by the artifacts that were buried with him.

The fluorine test was one of the devices which finally

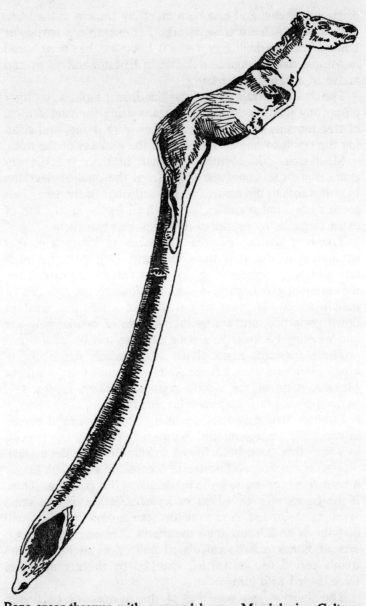

Bone spear-thrower with a carved horse—Magdalenian Culture

shattered the claim of 'Piltdown Man' to be a genuine ancestor of man. Dr Kenneth Oakley proved that the skull had been doctored to match the Sussex gravel in which it had been found (after being planted first), and was not nearly as old as it was originally thought to be; he also found that the jaw was that of a modern ape. On the other hand, the fluorine test helped to prove that the skull of 'Swanscombe Man' was found in gravel that was more than 100,000 years old and could be considered genuine. The method does not work in limestone soils because calcite prevents the fluorine from spreading in the bone tissue.

One of the newest methods of establishing the age of organic matter from the distant past is called the Carbon 14 Method, or the Radioactive Carbon Test.

The basic ingredient of all animal and vegetable life is carbon, and as carbon dioxide it is one of the chief constituents of air. Carbon consists of three distinct substances. They cannot be distinguished chemically, but each has a different atomic weight: 12, 13 or 14—and Carbon 14 is radioactive. It is formed when the carbon dioxide of the air is bombarded by cosmic rays from outer space and is changed from Carbon 12 to Carbon 14. All living plants and animals contain this radioactive substance. When they die it begins to decay, and does so at a steady rate.

In 5,568 (plus or minus 30) years—though scientists are beginning to think that this number is not quite accurate—half of it will have gone. This is called its 'half-life'. In 11,140 years half of what was left will have gone, and so on. A specially adapted Geiger counter can measure the amount of Carbon 14 in burnt organic matter, and with a margin of a hundred years or so on either side the age of the material can be determined. A tree cut down 5,568 years ago would produce only half as many clicks on a Geiger counter as a tree cut down yesterday.

One drawback to the method is that the material must be burnt to reduce it to sooty carbon; and sometimes it is not possible to sacrifice even part of a valuable find. The

Carbon 14 Test is most useful for objects which are between 5,000 and about 70,000 years old. The amount of Carbon 14 in anything older is too small to measure.

Another method of dating is by archaeomagnetism, again not so formidable a word as it sounds. You know that iron is especially affected by the north magnetic pole. A compass needle swings in that direction; so does a needle floating in water. Many rocks, including clay, contain oxides of iron and are thus magnetized, though not very strongly. The magnetism decreases when the iron is heated, and eventually it vanishes at a temperature of between 580 and 670 degrees Centigrade. This is called the Curie point. When the iron is cooled below the Curie point it becomes re-magnetized at its present strength and direction towards the magnetic north. But this new direction is not the same as the original direction, for the magnetic pole position changes from year to year, and in some parts of the world this variation can be measured to give its position over a few thousand years.

The difference between the two readings of the magnetic fields, one before the heating and cooling, the other after, is the basis on which the date of, for example, a piece of fired clay taken from a pottery kiln can be arrived at.

These are some of the ways in which the scientist has come to the aid of the archaeologist. Many other laboratory techniques are being tried out. They are too complicated to be described briefly, but the young archaeologist who is also scientifically minded will have a fascinating time trying to understand the principles behind them.

Botanists, chemists, physicists—they are all providing the archaeologist with these wonderful new techniques. The wise archaeologist accepts them gratefully, but with caution. For there is a danger in the invasion of archaeology by science. We must never forget that the object of archaeology is to *write history*, an art which must not be smothered by technology. We do not want the things in history which cannot be measured, weighed, poked and prodded, such as art and religion, to be neglected for the things that can.

MORE BOOKS ABOUT ARCHAEOLOGY

ATKINSON, R. J. C.: *Stonehenge* (H. Hamilton, 1956)

BACON, EDWARD: *Digging for History* (A. and C. Black, 1960)

BRION, MARCEL: *Pompeii and Herculaneum* (Elek, 1960)

BRODRICK, ALAN HOUGHTON: *Man and his Ancestry* (Hutchinson, 1960)

BRUCE-MITFORD, R. L. S. (Ed): *Recent Archaeological Excavations in Britain* (Routledge and Kegan Paul, 1956)

CARRINGTON, RICHARD: *A Million Years of Man* (Weidenfeld and Nicolson, 1963)

CERAM, C. W.: *Gods, Graves and Scholars* (Gollancz, 1952)

CHADWICK, JOHN: *The Decipherment of Linear B* (Penguin, 1961)

CLEATOR, P. E.: *The Past in Pieces* (Allen and Unwin, 1957)

CONTENAU, G.: *Everyday Life in Babylon and Assyria* (Edward Arnold, 1954)

COTTRELL, LEONARD: *The Bull of Minos* (Evans, 1955)
The Mountains of Pharaoh (Hale, 1956)
The Lost Pharaohs (Evans, 1950)
Wonders of Antiquity (Longmans, 1960)
The Anvil of Civilization (Faber, 1958)
(Ed.) *The Concise Encyclopaedia of Archaeology* (Hutchinson, 1960)

DANIEL, GLYN: *The Idea of Prehistory* (Penguin, 1964)

DEUEL, LEO (Ed.): *The Treasures of Time* (Souvenir Press, 1962)

FOX, P.: *Tutankhamun's Treasure* (O.U.P., 1951)

GREEN, CHARLES: *Sutton Hoo* (Merlin Press, 1963)

183

GRIGSON, GEOFFREY: *Painted Caves* (Phoenix House, 1957)

HILL, WILLIAM THOMPSON: *Buried London* (Phoenix House, 1955)

JESSUP, RONALD: *The Story of Archaeology in Britain* (Michael Joseph, 1964)

JOHNSTONE, PAUL: *Buried Treasure* (Phoenix House, 1957)

KENYON, KATHLEEN M.: *Beginning in Archaeology* (Phoenix House, 1961)

KRAMER, S. N.: *History begins at Sumer* (Thames and Hudson, 1958)

LAMING, ANNETTE: *Lascaux* (Penguin, 1959)

LLOYD, S. H. F.: *Foundations in the Dust* (Penguin, 1955)

MELLERSH, H. E. L.: *From Ape Man to Homer* (Hale, 1962)

MERTZ, BARBARA: *Temples, Tombs and Hieroglyphs* (Gollancz, 1964)

PALMER, GEOFFREY: *Quest for the Dead Sea Scrolls* (Dobson, 1964)

PALMER, GEOFFREY & LLOYD, NOEL: *Quest for Prehistory* (Dobson, 1965)

PAYNE, ROBERT: *The Gold of Troy* (Hale, 1959)

SHIPPEN, KATHERINE B.: *Men of Archaeology* (Dobson, 1964)

VAUGHAN, AGNES CARR: *The House of The Double Axe* (Weidenfeld and Nicolson, 1959)

VON HAGEN, VICTOR W.: *The Ancient Sun Kingdoms of the Americas* (Thames and Hudson, 1962)

WEBSTER, GRAHAM: *Practical Archaeology* (A. and C. Black, 1963)

WHEELER, LADY (Ed.): *A Book of Archaeology* (Cassell, 1957)

WHEELER, SIR MORTIMER: *Archaeology from the Earth* (Penguin, 1956)

WOOD, ERIC S.: *Collins Field Guide to Archaeology in Britain* (Collins, 1963)

WOOLLEY, SIR LEONARD: *Excavations at Ur* (Benn, 1954)
History Unearthed (Benn, 1958)
Digging up the Past (Penguin, 1960)
184

INDEX

185